THE RELIEF OF CHITRAL

First published 1910
This edition published by Lector House in 2024

ISBN: 978-93-6138-359-5

Lector House LLP
Registered Office: H. No. 96, Block C, Tomar Colony,
Burari, Delhi – 110084, India
info@lectorhouse.com
www.lectorhouse.com

THE RELIEF OF CHITRAL

FRANCIS EDWARD YOUNGHUSBAND,
GEORGE JOHN YOUNGHUSBAND

2024

LECTOR HOUSE LLP

Lieutenant Peterson. Lieutenant Jones. Lieutenant Moberly.
Surgeon-Captain Luard. Surgeon-Captain Browning Smith.

Colonel Kelly and his Officers. *[Frontispiece*

Lieutenant Stewart, R.A. Lieutenant Beynon. Colonel Kelly. Captain Borrodaile.
Lieutenant Cobbe. Lieutenant Bethune. Sergeant Reeves.

THE RELIEF OF CHITRAL

BY

CAPTAIN G. J. YOUNGHUSBAND
QUEEN'S OWN CORPS OF GUIDES
AUTHOR OF "EIGHTEEN HUNDRED MILES ON A BURMESE TAT";
"FRAYS AND FORAYS"; "THE QUEEN'S COMMISSION," ETC., ETC.

AND

COLONEL SIR FRANCIS YOUNGHUSBAND
K.C.I.E.
INDIAN STAFF CORPS
(LATE POLITICAL OFFICER IN CHITRAL)

WITH MAP AND ILLUSTRATIONS

PREFACE

This book is the joint production of two brothers, who are constantly being mistaken for one another, who happened to be present together in the same campaign and to both act as correspondents of the *Times* in that campaign. The chapters (III. IV. and V.) on Sir Robert Low's advance are by Captain George Younghusband, who was present throughout the operations on General Low's Staff. The remaining chapters are by Captain Francis Younghusband, who from his two years' residence in Chitral was better acquainted with the country through which Colonel Kelly marched his troops, and with the place in which the defence was made.

This record of the Chitral campaign is based on the official despatches published in the Gazette of India and in the Blue Book on Chitral affairs lately presented to the Houses of Parliament, and the management of the *Times* have kindly allowed that use should be made of the letters which the authors wrote to the *Times*.

The illustrations are from photographs taken by Sergeant Mayo, of the Photographic Section of the Bengal Sappers and Miners, which accompanied General Low's column; and from sketches very kindly furnished by Surgeon-Captain Browning-Smith and Lieutenant Beynon, who served with Colonel Kelly's Column.

October 1895.

A few verbal corrections and some slight additions have been made to bring this book up to date.

July 1910.

CONTENTS

LIST OF ILLUSTRATIONS

Page

CHITRAL EXPEDITION 1895.

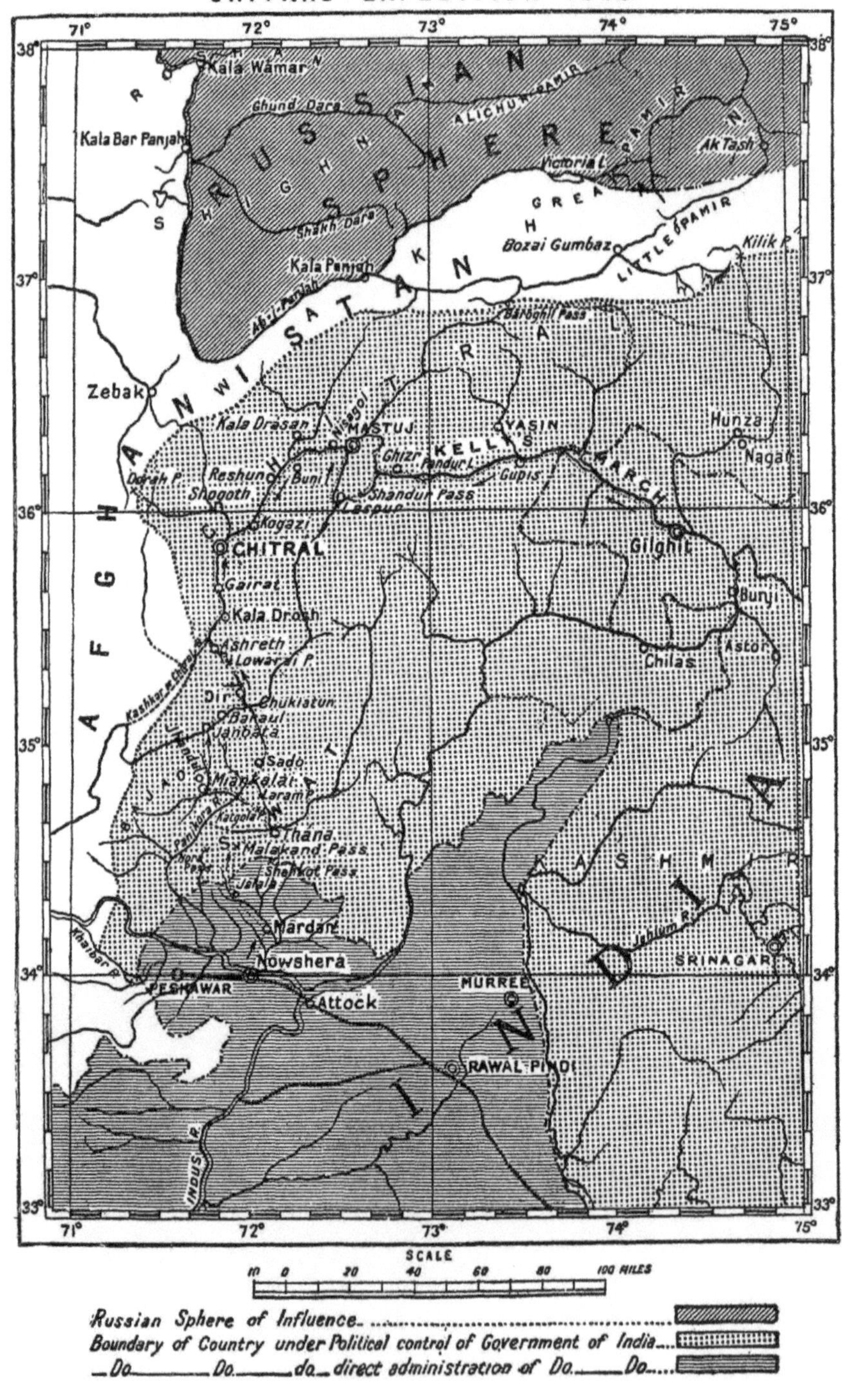

Map of Chitral Expedition 1895.

CHAPTER I

THE CAUSES OF THE WAR

In the middle of March of the year 1895, people in England were suddenly made aware that grave trouble had arisen upon the northern frontier of India; that the representative of the British Government was besieged in the heart of a mountainous country, hundreds of miles from the nearest support; and that operations on a large scale were contemplated by the Government of India to effect his release, and restore British prestige. Some account of how this trouble arose is required, and of the causes which necessitated this campaign by which the honour of the British name was saved, and British officers were rescued from an untimely end.

India is bounded on the north by successive ranges of mountains of great height, and among these mountains is the State of Chitral, a country somewhat larger than Wales, and supporting a population of 70,000 or 80,000 rough, hardy hillmen. Both the capital and the state itself are called Chitral, and the principal place, where is the fort of Chitral, is situated at a distance of about forty-seven miles from the main water-shed of the range of the Hindu Kush, which divides the waters flowing down to India from those which take their way into the Oxus, and on to Turkestan and Central Asia. Chitral is an important state, because of its situation at the extremity of the territory over which the Government of India exerts its influence, and for some years past, it had been the object of the policy of the Government of India, to control the external affairs of Chitral, in a direction friendly to our interests; to secure an effective guardianship over its northern passes; and to keep watch over what goes on beyond those passes. With these objects in view, Major Biddulph was sent to the country in 1877, and the first attempt was made to enter into relations with the Ruler or Mehtar of the country. No very definite arrangement was come to at this time, but in 1885, when war between Russia and England was imminent, Lord Dufferin despatched Sir William Lockhart at the head of an important mission to enter into more definite and complete relations with the Mehtar, and to report upon the defences of the country. Colonel Lockhart spent more than a year in Chitral and the neighbouring states on the north, as well as on the south side of the Hindu Kush range, and from that time to this the relations of the Government of India with the Rulers of Chitral have been of a close and intimate nature. Chitral was then governed by old Aman-ul-Mulk, a strong, astute ruler, who, by the force of his character, by intriguing, by murdering those of his rivals whom he could ensnare with his wiles, and by fighting the remainder, had consolidated a number of small states incessantly at warfare with one another into the Chitral of the year of the campaign. Under his firm rule, the country was held together, and, so long as he lived, no one dared to rise against him, or dispute his authority. But he had seventeen sons, and those who knew the customs of Mohammedan countries foresaw that, on his death, these must infallibly commence a fratricidal struggle for the throne.

At the end of August 1892, old Aman-ul-Mulk died, and the long-expected scramble for the Mehtarship immediately commenced. Of the seventeen sons, there were two who by reason of the rank of their mother, were regarded as having the strongest claims to the Mehtarship. These two youths had been invited down to India on a visit to the Viceroy some years before, and they were in receipt of small subsidies from the Government of India. Nizam-ul-Mulk was the name of the elder, and the younger was named Afzul-ul-Mulk. At the time of the old Mehtar's death, the second son happened to be in Chitral, while his elder brother was away in Yasin, 160 miles distant, carrying out his duties as Governor of that outlying province. Afzul-ul-Mulk immediately seized the arms and treasure in the fort, attached a large following to himself, for he was decidedly the more popular of the two brothers, and then proceeded to murder all those of his other brothers who, in spite of their lower birth, might certainly be expected to make a bid for the throne. He killed a number of these, and then set off with an army to fight his elder brother, Nizam-ul-Mulk, in Yasin. Afzul was a bold and daring leader, while Nizam was never noted for his courage, and had none of his brother's personal popularity. He was therefore only able to make a very feeble show of resistance, and he then fled to Gilgit, to the head-quarters of the political agent, and of the troops stationed there for the protection of this part of the Indian frontier, to seek refuge under British authority.

Afzul-ul-Mulk returned to his capital elated and triumphant. He was recognised by all his people as the Mehtar of the country, and the Government of India, in accordance with their principle of recognising as ruler the man whom the people themselves chose, proceeded to congratulate him upon his accession to the throne of Chitral. The anticipated troubles seemed to have come to an end in the space of a very few weeks, and there appeared to be nobody now to oppose Afzul-ul-Mulk's rule. The British Government saw seated on the throne of this important state a man for whom British officers who had met him had considerable admiration, and a man who, having visited India, and become acquainted with our real strength and resources, and who was believed to be loyally attached to the alliance with the British Government, was likely to prove an almost model ruler for the country.

Everything then seemed to have settled down satisfactorily; but Afzul-ul-Mulk had only just received the recognition of the Government of India, and had not been two months on the throne, when without warning, and suddenly as the fall of a thunderbolt, appeared one upon the scene who, in the space of a single night, upset all these dreams of peace. Afzul-ul-Mulk had by one means and another ridded himself of those of his brothers who were likely to cause him trouble. He was reasonably safe as regards brothers, but there was an uncle who had been overlooked. This was Sher Afzul, who many years before had struggled for the throne with the old Mehtar, but who had long since been driven from the country, and forced to live in exile in Afghan territory. This prince suddenly appeared before the walls of the Chitral fort. He had successfully intrigued with a number of men in Chitral who were inimical to Afzul-ul-Mulk, and so secured an entrance to the country. The fort of Chitral is situated only forty-seven miles distant from the pass into Badakhshan, over which Sher Afzul advanced, and he had ridden rapidly in with a hundred or more of horsemen, collected a few followers on the way, killed the Governor of the valley through which he passed, and in the dead of night appeared before the walls of Chitral itself.

Success or failure now turned upon the action of a few hours. If he could gain an entrance to the fort, and hold it, he would secure the throne for himself; but if he were held at bay for even that one night, he could only expect to be swamped in the morning by the undoubtedly strong following of Afzul-ul-Mulk. Sher Afzul was making a bold and daring move, and fortune favoured his audacity. Afzul-ul-Mulk, hearing from the inside of the fort the clamouring at the gate as Sher Afzul appeared, rushed out to ascertain what was the matter. In so doing he exposed himself, was shot down, and died almost immediately.

One king being dead, the Chitralis, with that versatility of temperament so characteristic of them, immediately proceeded to recognise as their ruler the man who had killed him. In no other country is the principle, so dear to the heart of the British Government, of recognising the *de facto* ruler, more fully acted upon than in Chitral. There was now no attempt to turn the invader out of the country, and no one waited to call in from Gilgit the eldest son of their old ruler. The Chitralis simply recognised as their chief the man who was the last to say he intended to rule them. Sher Afzul was to be their Mehtar. They believed all the promises so utterly incapable of fulfilment which he made to them, and Sher Afzul, having now seized the rifles, ammunition, and treasure which had before been taken possession of by Afzul-ul-Mulk, assumed the reins of government, and by promising houses, lands, and fair wives to every one who asked for them, and by liberal gifts of money, speedily made himself the popular idol of the people. But his lease of power was a short one.

While these events were occurring, Nizam-ul-Mulk, the eldest son of the old Mehtar, had been living quietly at Gilgit, enjoying a daily allowance from the British Government. He had seen his younger brother succeed to the throne, and recognised as Mehtar by the Government of India, and his fortunes for the time seemed at their lowest ebb, but in these turbulent countries, where the wheel of fortune turns so rapidly, no claimant to a throne need despair, however remote his chances of succeeding may seem for the time. And now Nizam-ul-Mulk, hearing of the death of his younger brother, at once plucked up courage to make an attempt to gain the throne of Chitral. He wrote to Colonel Durand, the British agent at Gilgit, asking him for his support, and saying that, should he become Mehtar, he would agree to British officers being stationed in Chitral, and to the establishment of a telegraph line, and would carry out all the wishes of Government. Nizam also signified his intention of moving against Sher Afzul; and having come to Gilgit of his own accord, and being there as our guest and not under detention,

Colonel Durand was unable to refuse him permission to leave Gilgit, and accordingly allowed him to go, while he despatched 250 rifles, 2 guns, and 100 levies, into the province of Yasin, in order to strengthen his own position, in the event of its becoming necessary to treat with Sher Afzul, and to preserve order in the western part of the Gilgit district and in Yasin.

Nizam-ul-Mulk on crossing the frontier, was joined by a large number of men from the upper valleys of Chitral, with whom he had been brought up as a youth, and who were always much attached to him, A force of 1,200 men, which Sher Afzul sent to oppose him, also went over to him, and he immediately marched on Mastuj, which he occupied without difficulty. Drasan fell into his hands on the 1st of December, and Sher Afzul, seeing the game was up, fled as rapidly as he had appeared, back into Afghan territory; where he remained, till at the commencement of the present year he again appeared upon the scene to set the whole of Chitral once more in a ferment.

Nizam-ul-Mulk felt that his success had been very largely due to the countenance which had been given him by the British authorities, and his first act on ascending the throne was to ask that a British officer might be sent to remain by his side. The Government of India directed that a mission under the charge of Surgeon-Major Robertson, and which consisted of Lieutenant The Honourable C. G. Bruce, Lieutenant J. H. Gordon, and myself, with fifty men of the 15th Sikhs should be deputed to proceed to Chitral to congratulate the new Mehtar on his succession, and to promise him the same subsidy and support as were given to his late father.

In the middle of January 1893, we crossed the Shandur Pass, 12,400 feet high, since rendered famous by the march of Colonel Kelly's column across it, and, in spite of the severity of the weather and the extreme cold, reached Chitral without mishap on the 25th of January. Here the mission remained till May, giving to the Mehtar that support which he so much required in the consolidation of his rule. Dr. Robertson and Lieutenant Bruce returned to Gilgit at the end of May, while Lieutenant Gordon and myself, with the whole of the escort, remained on in Chitral. As the months went by, the Mehtar gradually strengthened his position, and at the end of September, we were able to withdraw to Mastuj, a place sixty-five miles nearer Gilgit, which the Government of India desired should in future be the head-quarters of the political agent. During the following year, no event of importance occurred upon this frontier, though the restless Pathan chief, Umra Khan, the Mehtar's neighbour on the south, was constantly causing trouble by attacking the villages considered by the Mehtar to belong to Chitral. In the autumn of last year the Honourable George Curzon, M.P. (now Lord Curzon) entered Chitral territory from the direction of the Pamirs. He and I rode down together to the Mehtar's capital, and were received by him with every mark of hospitality. We had long conversations together, we dined with him and he with us, and we played polo together; and when on the 11th of October we rode away from Chitral, no one would have supposed it possible that in a few months' time the country, which then seemed so quiet, should be the scene of the bloody conflict which raged there in the first months of the ensuing year.

Nizam-ul-Mulk was by no means a pattern ruler, but, though deficient in courage, and unpopular with many of his people on account of his avaricious habits, was in many respects a good ruler, and he was certainly a firm ally of the British Government. He had been to India, had mixed with British officers, and had suffered adversity. At the same time he had no wild ambitions to lead him astray. His ruling passion was love of sport; and as long as he had the support of the Government of India to guard him from outside troubles, he felt that he could indulge his inclinations in that respect to his heart's content. The result, both to ourselves and to the Chitralis, was certainly satisfactory. The Chitralis were free from any gross oppression or misgovernment, they could enjoy life in their easy-going way as they would wish, and they could be ruled by their own ruler. At the same time, we had never to fear that the Mehtar would not be guided by us in any matter relating to his external affairs.

When, therefore, on the first day of January of the following year Nizam-ul-Mulk was shot dead while out hawking, by the directions of his half-brother, Amir-ul-Mulk, a characterless youth of about nineteen, every one who knew the country felt that a grave misfortune had occurred. At a stroke this miserable boy was able to sweep away the good results of two years' careful thought on the part of the Government and of their local officers, and to transform a peaceful state into the scene of a desperate struggle. The youth who had shattered the promising fabric, which had slowly been set up, was a son of the old Mehtar by one of his four legitimate wives, and Nizam-ul-Mulk would have liked to have murdered him, knowing that if he did not do so he ran the risk of himself being murdered by the youth. But knowing how averse the British authorities were to these murders, he had refrained from carrying out what he knew to be a prudent measure of self-defence, and he had now suffered for his leniency and his loyalty to the wishes of his allies.

At the time of this unfortunate occurrence, Lieutenant B. Gurdon, who had succeeded me a few weeks before in the political charge of Chitral, was on a visit to the capital with an escort of eight Sikhs: the remainder of his escort of 100 men being posted at Mastuj, sixty-five miles north-east of Chitral. Amir-ul-Mulk immediately sent a deputation to him asking to be recognised as Mehtar; and it is significant of the prestige and authority which we then enjoyed, that a reckless youth, in the very excitement of his impetuous action, should have come cringing in to a young British officer with only eight native soldiers at his back, asking for his countenance and support. Lieutenant Gurdon told him that he could merely refer the matter to the Government of India and await their orders. This Lieutenant Gurdon now did, but it may be imagined that his position at this time was one of considerable anxiety which required all the tact and coolness which he now proved himself to possess. He had at once sent for a reinforcement of fifty Sikhs from his escort at Mastuj, and these reached him on the 8th; and that they were able to do so, and were not hindered or molested on the way, is another sign that at that time there was no defined spirit of hostility to the British.

The Westminster Abbey of Chitral.

Where the Mehtars are buried.

Photo A. Esmé Collings. *W. Brighton.*

Lieutenant B. E. M. Gurdon, D.S.O.

In anticipation of trouble, however, 100 men were sent to reinforce Mastuj, 200 men were marched to Ghizr, and in the middle of January Surgeon-Major Robertson, the British agent at Gilgit, started for Chitral to report on the situation. Mr. Robertson arrived in Chitral at the end of January, and afforded timely relief to Mr. Gurdon, who, in the meantime had, in the words of the despatch of the Government of India on the subject, acted with admirable coolness and judgment, occupying a house in an excellent position for defence, if necessary, and quietly laying in supplies in case of trouble.

Meanwhile Umra Khan, chief of the Jandul State, immediately bordering Chitral on the south, had taken the opportunity which the troubles which were occurring in Chitral afforded to invade the country, ostensibly with the object of supporting Amir-ul-Mulk, but with the real intention of annexing it to his own dominions. This enterprising chief was the son of the ruler of the little Pathan State of Jandul, who, on the death of his father in 1879, had made an attempt to seize the throne from his eldest brother, but not being successful had prudently retired on a pilgrimage to Mecca. Having plucked up heart again two years later, he murdered his brother, seized the throne, and then commenced a series of wars against his neighbours, which only culminated in the disasters of the present year. Valley after valley he annexed to his country. Scarcely a month passed by without a fight, and with each success his ambitions only grew wider and stronger. His, indeed, was one of those uncontrollable spirits which feed upon high adventure, and tire of nought but rest.

He now thought he saw his opportunity of acquiring the more important and larger state of Chitral. He had dreamed one night that this should be his, and, to the excitable imagination of an Oriental, it seemed that his dream was a prophetic inspiration from on high. He was, undoubtedly, an accomplice with Amir-ul-Mulk in the murder of the late Mehtar; but it is not so certain whether he had done more than give that youth a general assurance that if he would murder the Mehtar he should be supported. Umra Khan at the time of Nizam's murder was preparing for an expedition elsewhere, and, had he been in direct communication with Amir-ul-Mulk as to the precise time of the murder, it is questionable whether he would have chosen the season of the year when the high pass between his own and Chitral territory was blocked with snow. However, seeing that the murder had occurred, and knowing that all the leading men in Chitral had previously been made away with, that the country had now no leaders, and must of necessity be split up into a number of opposing factions, he, without a moments hesitation, seized the opportunity, and in spite of the heavy snow on the pass, 10,000 feet in height, which separated him from Chitral, marched with 3,000 men into that country.

The Chitralis at first opposed this Pathan force. They had always looked upon the Pathans as their hereditary enemies, and had on many previous occasions resisted invasions by them. Had they now had any leader to keep them together, and to encourage them, the Chitralis would have been able to repulse the invaders. Could the British have supported them in their resistance, as Lieutenant Gurdon did with a few men in one of the preliminary skirmishes, they would have gained heart, and, with the spirit which they are capable of showing when once they are fairly aroused, would have beaten back Umra Khan's men; but Amir-ul-Mulk, their would-be leader, was incapable of exercising authority. He had not been recognised by the British officers as Mehtar, and it was doubtful whether he ever would be; and his hope lay therefore more with Umra Khan than with the British, and the British officers were unable to support the Chitralis in a quarrel of their own with this neighbouring chief without the direct instructions of their Government.

The resistance of the Chitralis therefore collapsed, Umra Khan succeeded in capturing Kila Drosh, the principal fort on the southern frontier of Chitral, and this he immediately commenced to strengthen, so as to form of it a firm "pied-à-terre" on Chitral territory. And just as affairs had taken this unfavourable turn, just when the Chitralis were divided and leaderless, when their country had an invader in its midst, once more appears upon the scene that evil spirit of Chitral and persevering aspirant for its throne, Sher Afzul. Scarcely more than two years previously he had killed one Mehtar, ruled the country for a month, and then been ousted by the elder brother, and now, after a further sojourn of two years in Afghan territory, in a confinement which the Amir of Kabul had most solemnly declared to the Government of India would be permanent, so that he might never again be allowed to disturb the peace of Chitral, he was allowed to escape from Afghan territory and join Umra Khan at Drosh in the latter half of February.

Mr. Robertson did not receive reliable information of his arrival in Chitral territory until the 24th of February, when he at once entered into communication with him. On the 27th of February, Mr. Robertson received from Sher Afzul a demand that he should go back to Mastuj at once. Sher Afzul promised to be friends with the Government on the same terms as previous Mehtars of Chitral, that is to say, that he was to receive subsidies from the Government, but that no British officer should reside in the country. But his promise was coupled with the threat that if his terms were not accepted, Umra Khan would at once advance. The two princes had, in fact, made an alliance, the basis of which was really hostility to the British Government. They were to induce or force the British officers from Chitral territory, and after that had been effected, they could then decide who should rule the country, one thing only being certain, that whoever should be the nominal Mehtar, Umra Khan would be the ruler practically. Mr. Robertson replied to Sher Afzul that the Maharajah of Kashmir was the Suzerain of Chitral, and that neither Umra Khan nor any one else could impose a Mehtar on Chitral without the permission of the Government; he added that Sher Afzul was wanting in respect to the Government of India, that he was informing the Government of Sher Afzul's demands, and would communicate their instructions to him, and that if in the meantime he attempted any overt act of hostility, he must take the consequences on his own head.

At the end of February, the Chitralis were still holding a position a dozen miles below Chitral, and Umra Khan was rapidly completing his preparations for the defence of Kila Drosh against an attack from the Chitralis, which he believed to be imminent. A few Chitralis of the lower class had gone over to Sher Afzul, but the principal men, though suspected of being partisans of Sher Afzul, did not openly defect. Suddenly, however, they now changed their minds and went over in a body to Sher Afzul. In that versatile and impulsive way so characteristic of them, they turned completely round, and, in place of joining the British and opposing Umra Khan, they now, under the impression that Umra Khan was the stronger, because the nearer power, and that the British were the weaker, because the more distant, joined the Pathan chief, and came surging on in a wave towards the fort of Chitral, which Mr. Robertson, with the escort of 400 men, which he had brought with him, had now occupied.

Amir-ul-Mulk had been deposed and was under the custody of the British officers, and Mr. Robertson had formally recognised Shuja-ul-Mulk, an intelligent, trustworthy little boy, nine or ten years old, as provisional Mehtar of Chitral, pending the orders of the Government of India.

On the 3rd of March, the combined Chitrali and Pathan forces appeared before Chitral, an action took place in which one British officer was mortally wounded, and another severely wounded, in which a General and a Major and twenty-one non-commissioned officers and sepoys of the Kashmir Infantry were killed, and twenty-eight wounded. The British force was then shut up within the walls of the fort, and no further news of them reached the Government of India for many weeks to come.

Information of the serious turn which affairs had taken in Chitral was received by the Government on the 7th of March, and they immediately decided that preliminary arrangements should be undertaken, in order to be prepared if necessary to operate against Umra Khan from the direction of Peshawur. It was believed that the garrison in the Chitral fort could resist an attack from Umra Khan and Sher Afzul's forces, and hold out as long as their ammunition and supplies lasted; but as communications were all interrupted, and as retreat was cut off, it appeared imperative that no effort should be spared to effect their relief by the end of April, if the investment was not otherwise removed before that date. On the 14th of March, in order that Umra Khan might have distinct notice of the decision to which the Government of India had thus come, a final letter of admonition was sent to him recounting the various warnings given to him against interfering with Chitral affairs, mentioning his various acts of aggression, directing him to at once quit Chitral territory, and telling him that if by the 1st of April he had not withdrawn, the Government of India would compel him to do so. The letter went on to say that the Government were making fresh preparations to send forward their forces for that purpose, and that he would only have himself to blame for any evil results that might fall upon him. At the same time a proclamation in the following terms was issued :—

To all the people of Swat and the people in Bajaur who do not side with Umra Khan.

Be it known to you, and any other persons concerned, that—

Umra Khan, the Chief of Jandul, in spite of his often repeated assurances of friendship to the British Government, and regardless of frequent warnings to refrain from interfering with the af-

> fairs of Chitral, which is a protected state under the suzerainty of Kashmir, has forcibly entered the Chitral valley, and attacked the Chitrali people.
>
> The Government of India have now given Umra Khan full warning that, unless he retires from Chitral by the 1st of April, corresponding with the 5th day of Shawal 1312 H., they will use force to compel him to do so. In order to carry out this purpose, they have arranged to assemble on the Peshawur border a force of sufficient strength to overcome all resistance, and to march this force through Umra Khan's territory toward Chitral.
>
> The sole object of the Government of India is to put an end to the present, and prevent any future, unlawful aggression on Chitral territory; and as soon as this object has been attained, the force will be withdrawn.
>
> The Government of India have no intention of permanently occupying any territory through which Umra Khan's misconduct may now force them to pass, or of interfering with the independence of the tribes; and they will scrupulously avoid any acts of hostility towards the tribesmen so long as they on their part refrain from attacking or impeding in any way the march of the troops. Supplies and transports will be paid for, and all persons are at liberty to pursue their ordinary avocations in perfect security.

Orders were also now issued for the mobilisation of the 1st Division of the Field Army under Major-General Sir Robert Low.

While preparations were in progress of this force, news reached the Government of India of the disaster to a detachment of troops under Captain Ross on their way to Chitral, when Captain Ross had himself been killed, his Lieutenant, Jones, been wounded, and fifty-six men killed out of a total of seventy-one; another detachment under Lieutenants Edwardes and Fowler was also known to be surrounded; and finally communication with the supporting post of Mastuj was severed. This intelligence materially altered the situation again. It was now known to the Government of India that before they had taken the action described above, Umra Khan and Sher Afzul had actually waged war upon British Indian and Kashmir troops.

The necessity for relieving the little garrison in Chitral was more imminent than had been supposed, while the reason for giving Umra Khan a period of grace within which he might withdraw from Chitral had now disappeared. Colonel Kelly, commanding the 32nd Pioneers, the senior military officer in the Gilgit district, was placed in command of the operations in the Gilgit district. His orders permitted him to make such dispositions and movements as he might think best, provided he undertook no operations which did not offer reasonable prospects of success. It was, however, felt that the relief of Chitral from the side of Gilgit was probably impossible. Gilgit is 220 miles from Chitral, and at this season of the year was cut off from all support from India, by passes 13,000 feet in height, which were now covered deep in snow, and which would not become available for the passage of troops till June. On the other hand, the road from Peshawur to Chitral was less than 200 miles in length, and on it there was only one pass of 10,000 feet which would still have snow upon it. This pass was not altogether impracticable for an army. Orders were therefore issued for the despatch of the Chitral Relief Force under Sir Robert Low, as soon as it could be made ready.

Before describing General Low's advance it is necessary to relate the circumstances under which the detachments under Captain Ross and Lieutenant Edwardes had, as mentioned above, suffered such signal loss.

CHAPTER II

CAPTAIN ROSS AND LIEUTENANT EDWARDES

On the 1st of March, while Mr. Robertson with his escort was in Chitral and active hostilities had not yet commenced, a native officer had started from Mastuj with forty men and sixty boxes of ammunition for Chitral. He had proceeded for a couple of marches and had reached Buni, when he found the road broken and rumours reached him that he was to be attacked. He accordingly wrote to Lieutenant Moberly, the special duty officer with the Kashmir troops in Mastuj, telling him of the state of affairs and asking for instructions. Rumours had by now reached Mastuj that Sher Afzul had entered Chitral territory and that large numbers of the Chitralis had joined him. But he was said to have friendly intentions towards the British and all the local head men reported to Lieutenant Moberly that no organised attack upon a party of troops was at all likely.

Still there was evidently a feeling of unrest abroad, and as a detachment of the 14th Sikhs under Captain Ross and Lieutenant Jones were now at Laspur, two marches on the Gilgit side of Mastuj, on their way up, Lieutenant Moberly wrote to ask Captain Ross to come on into Mastuj in a single march instead of two. This Captain Ross did, and on the evening of the 4th of March he started from Mastuj with fifty men to reinforce the Subadar, who was blocked at Buni. On the same day a detachment of twenty Sappers and Miners under Lieutenant J. S. Fowler, R.E., accompanied by Lieutenant S. M. Edwardes also arrived in Mastuj. The party were on their way to Chitral with engineering stores, and without halting at Mastuj they left on the following morning, March 5th, with the intention of overtaking the Subadar at Buni and with the combined party continuing the march to Chitral.

That evening Captain Ross returned to Mastuj reporting that everything was quiet at Buni, and that Lieutenants Edwardes and Fowler were to leave Buni on the 6th for Chitral with the ammunition escort. On the evening of March 6th Lieutenant Moberly received a note from Lieutenant Edwardes dated noon of the same day from Koragh, a small hamlet a few miles below Buni, saying that he heard he was to be attacked near Reshun, the first stage beyond Buni. Upon hearing of this Captain Ross at once moved from Mastuj, and also wrote to the officer commanding at Ghizr, the nearest post on the Gilgit side of the Shandur Pass, asking him to send up as many men as he could possibly spare to reinforce Mastuj. The strength of Captain Ross's party was

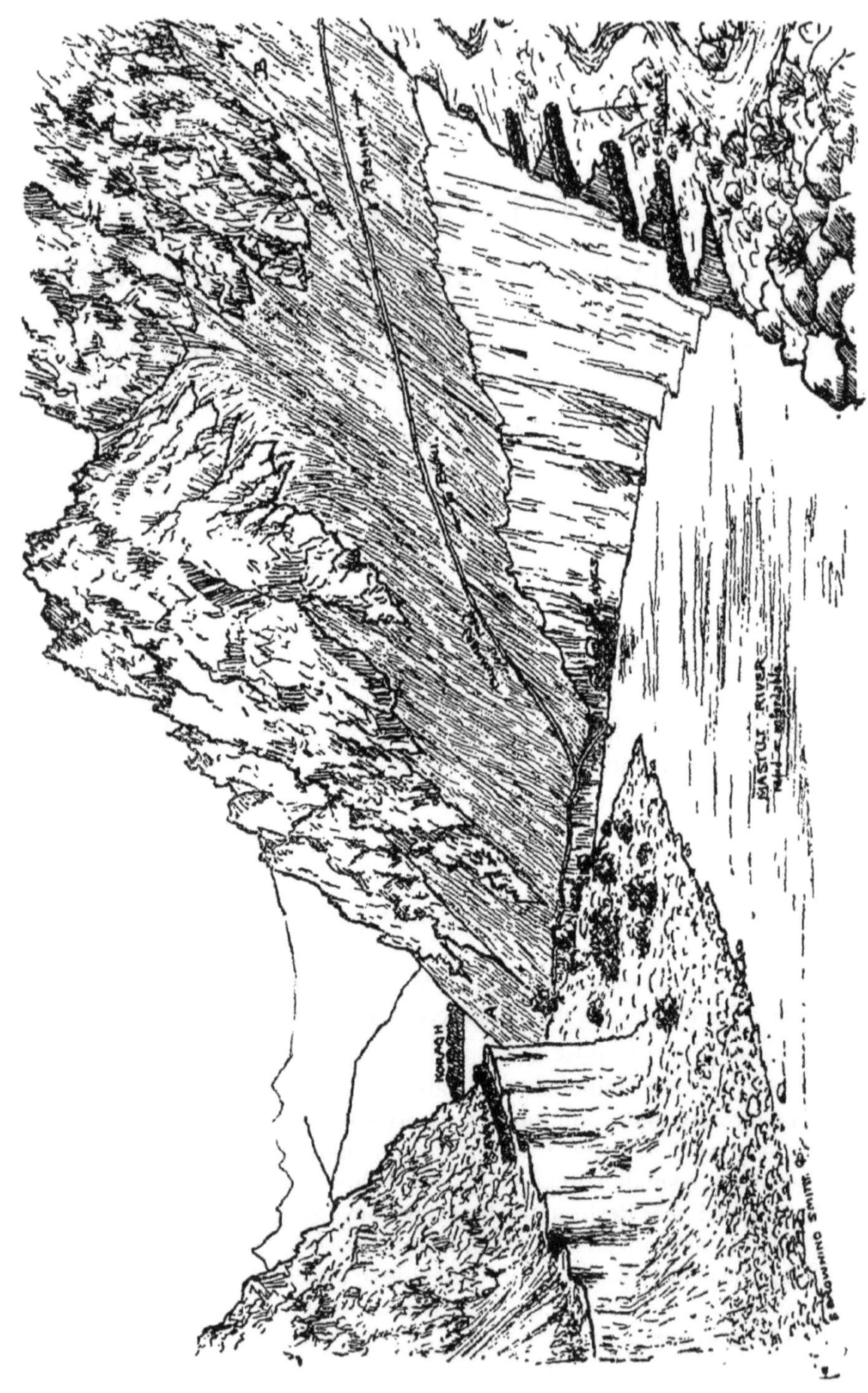

Diagrammatic Sketch of the Koragh Defile.

2 British Officers	8 Hospital followers
1 Native Officer	2 Cooks
6 Havildars (sergeants)	2 Water-carriers
3 Naiks (corporals)	1 Lascar
2 Buglers	1 Sweeper
82 Sepoys	2 Dhobis
1 Hospital-Assistant	

Nine days' rations and 140 rounds of ammunition per man were carried.

Leaving Mastuj on the morning of March 7th, Captain Ross reached Buni, eighteen miles distant, at 11 P.M. the same day. Here he left one native officer with thirty-three rank and file, while with the rest he and his subaltern, Lieutenant Jones, started for Reshun, the place, about thirteen miles lower down the valley, in which Lieutenant Edwardes' party were detained. Captain Ross's men took with them three days' cooked rations, and at about 1 P.M. the party reached the small hamlet of Koragh, about half way to Reshun, and a short halt was made here. What occurred after that may best be told in Lieutenant Jones's own words.

> About half-a-mile after leaving Koragh [he says] the road enters a narrow defile. The hills on the left bank consist of a succession of large stone shoots, with precipitous spurs in between; the road at the entrance to the defile for about one hundred yards runs quite close to the river; after that it lies along a narrow maidan, some thirty or forty yards in width, and is on the top of the river bank, which is here a cliff; this continues for about half-a-mile; then at the Reshun end it ascends a steep spur. When the advanced party reached about half way up this spur, it was fired on from a sangar which is across the road, and at the same time men appeared on all the mountain tops and ridges, and stones were rolled down all the shoots. Captain Ross, who was with the advanced guard, recalled the point of the advanced guard and fell back on the main body, with which I was. All our coolies dropped their loads and bolted as soon as the first shot was fired. Captain Ross, after looking at the enemy's position, decided to fall back upon Koragh, as it would have been useless to go on to Reshun, leaving an enemy in such a position behind us. With this object in view Captain Ross ordered me back with ten men to seize the Koragh end of the defile, to cover his retirement. By the time that I had reached within about one hundred yards of the sangar at this end I had only two sepoys left with me unwounded, and it was therefore impossible for me to proceed any further. I sent back and informed Captain Ross accordingly. Captain Ross in the meantime had occupied two caves in the river bank, and he ordered me to come back to him, which I did. Captain Ross then informed me that it was his intention to wait till the moon rose,

and that he would then try and force his way out. We stayed in the caves till about 8 P.M., and then we started to try and force our way out to Koragh.

When Captain Ross had got about half way across the stone shoot under the sangars at the Koragh end he decided to retire, as there was such a torrent of rocks coming down the shoot, that he thought that his party would be annihilated if he attempted to go on. Thereupon we again retired to the caves mentioned above. After reaching here, Captain Ross thought that he would try and get to the top of the mountain above us, and we started up the spur nearest above the caves. We had got some way up, when our road was completely barred by a precipice, and we could get no further, as we had no native of the country to guide us, and the ground was extremely dangerous. One of the sepoys, falling here, was killed. After looking about in vain for a path, Captain Ross again decided to retire to the caves, and we reached them about 3 A.M. As every one was now tired out, Captain Ross decided to remain here for the present. We remained in the caves all the day of the 9th. The enemy, meanwhile, did not molest us further than firing a few shots into the cave, and, as we had built up breast-works there, they could not do us much damage. During the 9th Captain Ross and myself both agreed that the only thing remaining for us to do was to cut our way out back to Koragh at all costs, and we decided to make the attempt about 2 A.M. On the 10th, when we thought that the enemy would least expect it, we started accordingly, and we attacked their sangars and drove them out of them; they retired a short distance up the hill and kept up a brisk fire from behind rocks. There was also a heavy fire kept on us from the sangars on the right bank of the river. A large number of sepoys were killed, or so severely wounded as not to be able to move, by the stones down the shoot which ran right into the river, and Captain Ross himself was killed in front of one of the sangars. I and seventeen rank and file reached the maidan on the Koragh side of the defile in safety, and when I got there I halted and re-formed the men, and stayed there some ten minutes, keeping up a heavy fire on the sangars on both banks of the river, in order to help any more of the men who could get through. While halting there, two bodies of the enemy's swordsmen attempted to charge us, but were checked by volleys and losing heavily. As the enemy now showed signs of again cutting our line of retreat, I considered that it was time to retire, especially as two more of my party were killed, and one mortally wounded, while I had been waiting here. Of the remaining fifteen, I myself and nine sepoys were wounded. We retired slowly to Buni, where we arrived about 6 A.M. It was quite impossible to bring any wounded men who were unable to walk with us, and it was equally impossible to bring their ri-

> fles, etc. Therefore a certain number, about forty of these, fell into the hands of the enemy. I estimate the enemy's numbers at about 1,000, and think that they must have lost heavily. I spent from the 10th to the 17th March at Buni, having occupied a house there and put it into a state of defence.

On the 17th he was relieved by Lieutenant Moberly, as will be subsequently told.

In concluding his report, Lieutenant Jones says that he cannot speak too highly of the steadiness and gallantry shown by the men of the detachment, whose behaviour throughout he considers above praise.

We now have to follow the fortunes of the party under Lieutenants Edwardes and Fowler, to whose assistance Captain Ross had set out. This party, as will be remembered, had marched from Mastuj on the 5th of March before any news of an outbreak of hostilities had reached that place. They were escorting ammunition and engineering stores for the troops at Chitral, and their party consisted of twenty Bengal Sappers and Miners, forty-two Kashmir Infantry, an orderly, three officers' servants, and two followers. On the 6th they reached Reshun, a large, but straggling village situated on a sloping plain between the left bank of the Chitral river and the steep mountain sides which rose behind. The houses are detached and dotted over the plain, each surrounded by an orchard. On the edge of a cliff which overhangs the river was a sangar, which the detachment now occupied, and here they stored their kit and ammunition, while a small party consisting of Lieutenants Edwardes and Fowler with twenty Bengal Sappers and Miners, and ten Kashmir Infantry started out to repair a break in the road a few miles below Reshun. Immediately after leaving the village the road to Chitral ascends a spur to a height of about 1,000 feet, and descending again to the level of the river passes for half-a-mile or so over a plain, and then enters a narrow defile with the unfordable river on one hand and inaccessible cliffs on the other.

The British officers were unaware, though the siege of Chitral had commenced three days ago, that the Chitralis had risen in arms against the British, but they saw sufficient evidence of a hostile spirit to induce them to take every precaution on entering this defile. All the hill-sides were carefully examined with telescopes, and, as some sangars were observed, Lieutenant Fowler was sent to scale the heights on the left bank so as from there to be able to look down into the sangars on the opposite bank. Meanwhile, Lieutenant Edwardes remained with the rest of the party close outside the defile. Lieutenant Fowler with some difficulty found a way up the hill-side, and was engaged in examining the opposite cliffs, when suddenly a shot came from them, and about two hundred men rushed out from a village where they had been concealed and began swarming into the sangars. Lieutenant Fowler kept up a heavy fire on them, as he was well above the sangars, and did considerable execution.

But the enemy had now begun climbing the hill-sides behind him so as to cut him off from Lieutenant Edwardes, and he was forced to retire. His position indeed was now a very precarious one, for the Chitralis had succeeded in getting above him, and were hurling down stones upon his party, besides firing upon them. Lieutenant Fowler himself was wounded in the back of the shoulder, the corporal of the party was also shot, and two other men wounded. Scrambling and jumping down he succeeded, however, in bringing his party with the wounded men down the hill-side again and on to the plain where Lieutenant Edwardes with the main body was covering his retreat. The Chitralis with Lieutenant Edwardes had been trying to induce him to enter the defile, in which case he would without doubt have suffered as Captain Ross's ill-fated party had done. But Edwardes had prudently waited till Fowler could report the hill-sides clear, and then, finding that instead of their being clear the enemy were now swarming on to them, he saw that his only plan was to retire to Reshun; and this, when Lieutenant Fowler had rejoined him, he accordingly did.

But they were nearly two miles from the village: they had an open plain to cross and the spur nearly a thousand feet high to climb. One British officer and several men were wounded, and the enemy were gaining ground along the hill-sides. Disaster seemed imminent, but by holding the crest of the spur, and by firing steadily on the enemy to keep them at a distance, the retirement was effected without serious loss, and the sangar near the village of Reshun, where the rest of the party had been left, was reached before the enemy could cut them off.

There is one little incident in this retirement which merits a very special mention. It has been said that Lieutenant Fowler was wounded. Now his pony was awaiting him in the plain at the foot of the hill-side up which he had been climbing; and as a steep hill, a thousand feet in height, had to be ascended on the way back to Reshun, it might have been supposed that Fowler would have mounted his pony and ridden up the hill. But there were also some sepoys wounded; and these in Fowler's opinion had to be looked after first. So he mounted a sepoy on his pony, and walked himself. It is not to be wondered at that when the native soldiers see their officers ready to make such sacrifices for them, they should be willing to follow them anywhere, and stand by them to the last, as indeed these very soldiers were now called upon to do.

For now the first blood was drawn the people rose excitedly and surrounded the little British party in the quarters they were occupying. The British officers found it impossible to hold the original sangar on the cliff by the river, for it was exposed to fire from the opposite bank, and had no head-cover. They therefore decided upon occupying some houses by the polo ground, the very spot where Mr. George Curzon and myself had camped without a single man as escort, only five months previously. In this batch of houses, cover and fire-wood could be obtained, and a certain amount of supplies also. The only drawback in occupying them was that they were more than a hundred yards from the river, and consequently there was considerable risk of their water supply being cut off. The officers hoped, however, to be able to keep the road to the river open by their fire.

Immediately upon returning to Reshun, the officers set to work to make the position defensible, and the following account of their brave resistance against overpowering numbers of the enemy is compiled from the report they subsequently submitted to Government. The first work to be done was the construction of sangars on the roofs of the houses (the houses being flat-roofed), the loopholing of the walls, blocking up entrances, and knocking out passages of communication. The materials available for making the sangars were the mud bricks of which the houses were built, roof timbers and other pieces of timber lying about, and boxes, grain bins, etc. An attack was fully expected that same night, and every possible precaution had to be taken before darkness set in. Before dusk the ammunition and the wounded had to be transported from the sangar near the river to the house. Some Kashmir sepoys volunteered for this work, and though they had to run the gauntlet of a heavy fire in crossing the space of a hundred yards which separated the sangar from the end of the garden-wall round the house, they carried it out without losing a single man. "Already dead tired, these men behaved splendidly," say the British officers in their report.

The enemy had been firing all day upon the party while they were at work, but at sunset their fire slackened and they went off to eat the evening meal, for this was the month of the Ramzan when Mohammedans have to fast all day and eat nothing between sunrise and sunset. Every man on the defending side was now posted in his place, and told to strengthen his cover for himself. And so the first night fell on the little party, now at bay, in the heart of an enemy's country, with their retreat cut off, and impossible defiles on either side of them. Out of the sixty-two men, they had already lost one corporal killed, two men mortally and eight others less severely wounded, and one of the two British officers was also wounded. The men had had hard work the whole day long, they had had no food and little water, and now at night they could take no rest, for the enemy commenced firing again, and the defenders had to expect a rush from the houses and garden walls close by at any moment. The defenders' position was indeed surrounded by these houses, walls, and trees, which gave ample cover to the enemy; and the demolition of these was undoubtedly a matter of the first importance. But beyond those immediately around the house, there was more cover occupied by the enemy's sharpshooters, and the British officers considered that it would have been too risky to have taken men from their places to demolish these, and so expose them where they might have been cut off at any moment. There was a difficulty, too, about burning the houses, for large quantities of kindling wood would have been required for the purpose, and from whichever side the defenders should burn fires, the enemy would attack from the other, and thus have them between themselves and the light.

All night long the garrison remained at their posts, and when day dawned on the morning of the 8th they were all utterly exhausted. But the fear of immediate attack being over, half the men were brought down from their posts, and a meal was cooked from the flour which had been found in the houses. Water, which had of course to be now carefully husbanded, was also served out; and after the men had refreshed themselves, they were allowed to sleep in turns. During the day the enemy kept up a continuous fire from sangars which they had thrown up on the hill-sides. At twilight the remainder of the baggage was brought in from the sangar, and the garrison then had to think of replenishing the water supply. Two large earthenware vessels were lashed on poles, and Lieutenant Fowler with the volunteers and a bhisti (water-carrier) set out for the river. The men carried water-bottles and the bhisti his mussuck (skin). Fortunately no enemy were met with, and the party were able to make two trips, and so fill up all the storage vessels at the disposal of the garrison.

That night, as on the previous one, the defenders stood to their posts expecting an assault at any moment; but the night passed by quietly until just before dawn on the morning of the 9th, when the moon had gone down and night was at its darkest. The enemy then charged down through the houses, and got behind the garden wall in large numbers. Lieutenant Edwardes and his party at once opened fire at about twenty yards range, while the enemy were shouting and urging each other on to the assault. There was a tremendous din of tom-toms as they were beaten furiously to encourage the assailants, but none of the men could approach to within twenty yards of the deadly fire poured out by the defenders, and as the dim light of early dawn grew clearer, it became evident to the garrison that the enemy had no stomach for further assault. Some Pathans among the assailants were still seen urging on the Chitralis and hurling abuse at the defenders, but at about 9 A.M. they all retired, and contented themselves for the rest of the day with beating tom-toms and howling in the village. During the attack the native soldiers of the defence showed the utmost steadiness, but four of them were killed and six others wounded. On account of the darkness, it was impossible to estimate the number of the enemy or their losses. But there must have been several hundreds, and a very large portion were armed with Snider and Martini-Henry rifles.

After the assault had been thus successfully repulsed water was served out, a meal was cooked, and the men allowed to sleep in turns. In the evening it was seen that the enemy had barred the road down to the water. At dusk the defenders still further strengthened their sangars, and fully expecting another attack, kept up a vigilant outlook. But "we and the men were terribly weary," say the officers, "and it was very difficult to keep the sentries awake, although they were posted double."

The night passed off quietly, however, and in the morning it was seen that the enemy had cleared off the hills, though sharpshooters still surrounded the defenders in sangars from fifty to two hundred yards distant. Lieutenant Edwardes dressed the wounded, who had so far only been bandaged. "Never a groan or complaint was heard," says the report, though there were no medical appliances, and though not sufficient water was available with which to thoroughly wash the wounds. Bandages, crutches, and splints had to be improvised, and the officers used a weak solution of carbolic and carbolic tooth-powder for the purpose of dressing the wounds. The corpses of the six dead men were also brought out and prepared for burning. At dusk an attempt was made to procure water again, and Lieutenant Fowler with twenty sepoys started down towards the river. But the enemy had now built and occupied sangars along the cliff at the river's edge, and the work of getting down to the river was one of extreme risk. Lieutenant Fowler succeeded in getting to within ten yards of the first sangar and within five yards of the sentry without being observed. About twenty men could be seen sitting round a fire in the interior with their rifles lying by their sides. A volley was poured into these men, and then Lieutenant Fowler charged down on the top of them. A few men only succeeded in escaping down the cliff to the river bed. Meanwhile the enemy in a second sangar, roused by the firing, lined the walls and began firing to their front. But Fowler had got round them behind a wall on their flank, and he now charged right up the wall, poured a second volley into these men over the fires, also knocked over about six of them, then bayoneted a few more, while the remainder fled. And so successful had Fowler been in surprising these parties, that not a single man of his was scratched. The way down to the water was open, but Fowler now heard heavy firing and the Pathan cry of attack in the direction of the post. So having collected his men, he retired at once to rejoin Lieutenant Edwardes. The enemy's attack was repulsed by this latter officer before Fowler's return, but the attempt to obtain water had to be abandoned for the night.

On the following day nothing of importance occurred, and that night the defenders succeeded in reaching the river and bringing back water, the supply of which was still further replenished by collecting the rain in waterproof sheets. A well was sunk to a depth of twelve feet, but as rock was then struck, the attempt to procure water in that manner had to be abandoned.

On the morning of the 13th a white flag was shown by the enemy, and a Pathan shouted out "Cease firing!" The defenders also hoisted a white flag, and sent out Jemadar Lal Khan to parley with the Pathan while every man stood to his post. After some talk, the Jemadar returned with the report that Mohamed Isa, Sher Afzul's right-hand man, had just arrived from Chitral with a following to stop the fighting and speak with the British officers. Lieutenant Edwardes sent word in reply that if Mohamed Isa would come to the defenders' side of a gap in the wall of the polo ground, situated only sixty yards from the wall of the houses held by the British officers, and entirely under fire from the defenders, one of the British officers would go out and meet him. Mohamed Isa agreed to do this: he came to the gap, and Lieutenant Edwardes then went out to talk with him, while Lieutenant Fowler remained inside the post with his men standing ready to arms in case of treachery.

When Lieutenant Edwardes met Mohamed Isa, that prince informed him that he had just arrived from Chitral, where Sher Afzul and Dr. Robertson were corresponding with a view to the former being recognised as Mehtar. Mohamed Isa said that all fighting had ceased, and that he was most anxious to be friends with the Indian Government. After some talk between the British officer and the Chitral prince, the conditions of an armistice were arranged, and it was stipulated that the British force should remain within their walls, that no firing should take place, that no Chitralis were to approach the walls, that water-carriers were to be allowed to go down to the river, and that supplies were to be provided by the Chitralis. Lieutenant Edwardes also wrote a letter to Dr. Robertson in Chitral, and to the officer commanding at Mastuj, stating in English that an armistice had been arranged, and adding in French what his losses had been, and expressing very great doubt of his being able to beat off any further assault. Having arranged these conditions, Lieutenant Edwardes returned to the post.

The bhistis were sent down to fetch water, and supplies were brought to the fort wall by the Chitralis. The night following passed in quiet, but vigilance was not relaxed. Rain fell heavily during the night, and a quantity of water was collected in waterproof sheets. In the afternoon of the 14th of March a further parley was asked for, and on the arrival of Mohamed Isa, accompanied now by another Chitrali prince named Yadgar Beg, at the former place of meeting, Lieutenant Edwardes again went out to confer with him, while Lieutenant Fowler remained, as before, inside the fortified post. Yadgar Beg confirmed to Lieutenant Edwardes the story previously told by Mohamed Isa, and both the princes were full of protestations of friendship. Yadgar Beg said he had a large following who desired to be friends, and not enemies, of the British. The same afternoon the bhistis were again sent to bring in water, and having to go some distance through the village, they reported that the houses were full of Pathans. They were not, however, ill-treated in any way, and Mohamed Isa sent in a sheep and other supplies to the British officers. Lieutenant Edwardes sent another letter to inform Dr. Robertson of the presumed strengthening of the enemy, and to let him know that the rations would not last beyond the 17th of March, *i.e.* three days hence.

So far the relations between the British officers and the Chitralis had been conducted upon an apparently friendly footing, the aim of the Chitralis being to lull the British into a sense of security. On the afternoon of the following day, the 15th of March, occurred that act of treachery by which the two officers were captured, and the greater number of their men lost their lives. In the afternoon, Mohamed Isa sent in word that now peace was restored, he and his men wished to amuse themselves, and he asked permission to play polo on the ground immediately outside the post which the British party were occupying. It seemed to the British officers that there could be no harm in granting this permission, for no man riding on the polo ground could escape their fire, and they therefore decided to grant Mohamed Isa's request. The Chitrali prince then sent to ask that both officers would come and look on, as so far he had only seen Lieutenant Edwardes. He also offered to lend the officers ponies on which to play polo. The British officers considered that as they had trusted the Chitralis so far, they might trust them further; so when Mohamed Isa and his men arrived upon the polo ground, both Lieutenant Fowler and Edwardes, having previously ordered their men to their posts which commanded the entire polo ground, went out to meet the Chitralis. A bedstead was placed in the gap in the wall of the polo ground, on the spot where the former meetings had taken place, and Mohamed Isa sat next to the officers until the men were ready to begin the game. The British officers were asked to play polo, but refused. Mohamed Isa, however, joined in the game, while Yadgar Beg sat with Edwardes and Fowler. A third arrival from Chitral, speaking to the British officers, confirmed the story of Mohamed Isa and Yadgar Beg, that peace between the British and the Chitralis had been made.

The polo ground at Reshun is about fifty yards broad and one hundred and twenty yards long, and slopes away from the post occupied by the British, the further side of the ground not being covered by the fire of the British garrison. Lieutenant Edwardes asked Mohamed Isa to order the men, who numbered about one hundred and fifty, and who were armed with rifles and swords, to go to the further side of the ground. The officers had some tea made and brought out for the Chitralis to drink. After the polo was over, Mohamed Isa asked if the men might dance, as is the custom of the country at the conclusion of a game. The British officers consented, and the dance began. Then under the excuse that there was a wet place in front of the officers, the bedstead on which they were seated was moved to the right, bringing it under cover of the end of the wall and the polo ground. The officers found it difficult to object to this, as it seemed impossible that any attempt at treachery could be unattended by heavy loss to the Chitralis. As the dance proceeded, more men began to collect and to press forward in a ring round the dancers, and the officers observed that a number had come over to the wall side of the polo ground. At a pause in the dance the officers stood up and said that they were tired, and would now go back to their post. On this Mohamed Isa himself suddenly seized the British officers, and a rush of men was made upon them, and they were dragged under cover of the wall. A volley was immediately fired by the British garrison; but the Chitralis kept under the wall, and none of them seemed to have been hit. Firing then became general for a short time, till it gradually died down into single shots fired at intervals. The officers in the meantime had their feet and hands bound, and were dragged by the legs along the ground away from the gap. All their buttons, badges, etc., were violently torn off and their pockets rifled, and Fowler's boots and stockings were taken off. In about half an hour the officers saw the enemy carry off some of their dead and wounded, and men came out laden with loot. They also saw at least one Kashmir sepoy being driven along with a load. With their arms still bound, the officers were taken off to the house in which Mohamed Isa lived, where they were seated in a verandah. What happened to the garrison of the post they could not at the time ascertain; but they subsequently met twelve of their men in Chitral, and it appears that the Chitralis rushed the place, killed numbers of the men, and carried these few off as prisoners.

In remarking upon the defence, the British officers say they had frequently considered the question of destroying a portion of the ammunition in their charge. This ammunition had now fallen into the hands of the enemy, and was a great advantage to them. It would have been well, therefore, if the British officers could have managed to have destroyed it; but they say that in the hurry of improvising the defence on the first night of the siege, they had been compelled to build the ammunition boxes up into a rude parapet, to afford a cover to their men. Subsequently these boxes had been covered up with beams, bricks, kits, and *débris*, and it was consequently very difficult to get them out without pulling down the cover so much needed. The moonlight nights, too, had rendered the removal of them very risky, as the long beams necessitated making large gaps, and any noise inside the post immediately drew the fire from the enemy, which was very effective in the moonlight. Moreover, the ammunition was intended for the use of local levies who were expected from Gilgit, and these levies without the ammunition would have been perfectly useless.

The British officers determined therefore to keep it till they could hold out no longer, and to then destroy it. Lieutenant Edwardes had also to consider the advisability of making sorties; but though he could have doubtless driven off the enemy for a time by such sorties, yet he recognised that he would have lost men in doing so, and with the small number at his disposal he could not afford to lose a single man.

The subsequent adventures of the two officers form a thrilling tale. After passing the night bound at Reshun, with a man holding on to a rope fastened to each of them, Lieutenant Fowler was sent towards Chitral, led at the end of a rope and under the escort of two Pathans and two Chitralis. On the following day Lieutenant Edwardes, who was at first to have been sent to Mastuj, was sent to join Lieutenant Fowler. On the way there they were met by a sergeant and ten men of Umra Khan, who, after quarrelling with the Chitralis, insisted upon taking them on as their prisoners. On the 19th of March the two officers reached Chitral, and were met there by a colonel and about a hundred men of Umra Khan's army. They were led into the presence of Majid Khan, Umra Khan's representative and half-brother, and now his successor in the rule of the Jandul State. The two officers were received civilly, and the Janduli prince expressed regret at the course of events, and of the treachery which had been practised on the British officers. He assured them of good treatment, and after a short interview the officers were marched with an escort of forty men to see Sher Afzul, the claimant to the throne of Chitral. The escort accompanied the British officers into the room in which they found Sher Afzul sitting, surrounded by a strong escort, and with a loaded rifle in his lap. He received the British officers civilly, and gave them tea and cakes. He also talked to them at great length of the negotiations which had taken place between him and Dr. Robertson. He further expressed sorrow at the treachery which had been used to them, and said that he would see to their comfort, and arrange supplies as far as possible, though supplies were difficult to obtain, as everything had been taken into the fort. Both Sher Afzul and Majid Khan, at the earnest request of Lieutenant Edwardes, promised to make strict search for all men of their party who might still be alive. The two officers were permitted to communicate with the British garrison besieged in the fort, but were not allowed to visit them. It was the object of the besiegers to let the defenders know, without doubt, the disaster which had befallen the British detachment, in order to depress as far as possible the spirit of the defence.

On the evening of March 20th, Lieutenants Edwardes and Fowler saw the native clerk of the political agent, who had been allowed to come out from the fort for the purpose of communicating with the officers, but all conversation had to be carried on in the presence of the Pathans and Chitralis. No talk in English was permitted, and the officers were only allowed to ask in Hindustani for clothing, plates, knives, forks, etc.

On the 21st of March the officers received from their beleaguered comrades in the fort some clothing and necessaries, and they again saw the political agent's native clerk in the presence of Sher Afzul and Majid Khan and others. These princes explained to the British officers their view of the situation, which was that they did not wish to fight the British if they would retire to Gilgit or Peshawur, and they asked Lieutenant Edwardes to ask one of the officers in the fort to come up and meet them. A letter was accordingly written to Lieutenant Gurdon inside the fort, telling him that if he met them under the walls of the fort they would give him some useful information. But no reply was received from Lieutenant Gurdon, and there is no doubt that the only object of the besiegers was to capture the other officers of the garrison in as treacherous a way as they had seized Lieutenants Fowler and Edwardes.

On the 24th of March the two captured British officers were sent towards Drosh to meet Umra Khan, the Pathan chief. Here on the following day they had a long interview with this important ruler. Umra Khan they found to be of a tall and manly appearance, with a straightforward, commanding manner of speaking, and with a great influence over his men. On these, and on all other occasions, he treated his captives with civility and consideration. He now gave them a choice of returning to Chitral, or of going with him to his native country of Jandul, some seven or eight marches to the south. As the chief would not allow the sepoys to go with the British officers to Chitral, they decided upon accepting the alternative of accompanying Umra Khan to Jandul, and started for that place on the following day.

Umra Khan had given orders that everything that could be obtained should be given to them before himself, but his followers did not carry out these orders, and the officers suffered much from bad food and bad quarters on the way. From the Chitral fort they had obtained a bag of sugar and a pound of tea, which they considered great luxuries, and they cooked food with the assistance of the sepoys who from Chitral onwards were accompanying them. The officers were never in any way threatened, but they knew that they were always liable to be killed by some fanatic who might have a blood feud against the British. A strong guard, armed with loaded rifles, accompanied them, however, and never for a moment allowed them to go more than a few yards from them, and this was doubtless as much for their protection as to prevent their escape. The guard always had in it some men who had served in our Indian army, and although many of them were extremely ruffian-like in appearance, and probably were thorough scoundrels, yet they mostly treated the officers in an easy and friendly manner, and were always willing to share with them the scanty rations they obtained on the march. The officers on the way occupied the ordinary country houses, which were very dark and dirty, and full of smoke and insects. The guard of ten men or more always slept and lived in the same room as the officers, and as most of them had colds and coughs, and were incessantly spitting on the floor, the prisoners had little quiet. The sepoy prisoners were given the same food as was served out to Umra Khan's men. But this ration on the march was a very small one.

The three Hindu prisoners were made to learn the Kalin, and their hair was cut; but they were not made to publicly declare themselves Mussulmans, and they never really changed their faith. No attempt was ever made to induce the officers to become Mohammedans, nor was any fanatical feeling displayed by the people whom they met. The men would eat the officers' bread, and gave them some of theirs. The Pathans would often ask the officers how they managed to exist without wine, and while in Chitral the officers were offered the contents of all the medicine bottles taken in the hospital outside the fort as a substitute. This delicate attention was however declined.

The prisoners were naturally an object of great curiosity to the people, and crowds gathered to see them. These people specially delighted to see the officers eat with knife and fork, and laughed at their attempts to eat with their fingers. This curiosity on the part of the populace the British officers found to be somewhat annoying, and the guard soon discovering that they did not like visitors at meal times, kept them off while the officers were eating; but at other times the prisoners received the public, and sat to be inspected whilst conversing with the people through interpreters. Umra Khan himself, as has been said, always treated his captives with civility, and was much interested in talking with them, and as long as he was with them and had leisure sent for them every day. He twice took them out hawking, and asked them to walk alongside him. The officers were not allowed to communicate with any one, except through the chief, nor were they allowed any writing materials, but they had obtained some paper and a pencil in Chitral and managed to keep a short diary of each day hid in their clothes. They were allowed to purchase materials with which to make clothes for themselves and their sepoys, and the traders gave them credit on their written acknowledgment.

Marching towards Jandul, the party on the 28th of March reached the Lowarai Pass, 10,000 feet in height, and now covered deep in snow. Leaving Ashreth, the last Chitrali village on the north side of the Pass, they ascended the deep narrow rocky valley to the Pass. At four miles from the summit they had to send back their ponies as the snow was now too soft to allow of their being taken over. They then had a very stiff pull up on foot, and on the top were caught in a violent storm of hail and snow. The wind was bitterly cold, and they were almost blinded by the driven snow. On the other side one of their sepoys complained of pain in the stomach, and he was left behind with another sepoy to look after him, but he died at night. Soon after dark the officers reached Dir, having marched twenty-four miles and crossed a difficult pass. Here at Dir, however, they were given better quarters and better food. On the 30th of March they marched to Barwa, Umra Khan's chief fort, crossing the Jhanbatai Pass, 7,000 feet high, from which they could obtain a view over the Pathan chief's own native valley. On the summit of the Pass, Umra Khan seated the British officers beside him, and, giving them food and sweetmeats, asked them how they liked his country. For a long time he sat there with the officers at his side gazing over his native valley stretched out at his feet, and then proceeding down the hill-side he was met by crowds of men on horseback and on foot as he marched into Barwa.

The officers remained here about a fortnight; but on the 1st of April the Mussulman sepoys were told that they could consider themselves at liberty, and the guard over them was removed. A native officer accordingly left and proceeded to Peshawur, where he brought the news of the disaster to his party.

The Lowarai Pass.

News now began to come in of the fighting between General Low's force and the Pathan tribes, and great excitement prevailed. Numbers of men began clearing out, taking all their goods with them to hide on the hill-sides. It is a remarkable point that as the panic increased, the officers received greater attention, and at the approach of our troops they were supplied with two fowls, flour, rice, butter and milk daily. On the 12th of April both of the officers were taken to Munda, Umra Khan's strongest fort. There they met a native political officer who had been sent by the British authorities to treat with Umra Khan. A long conversation took place between Umra Khan and the native official, the upshot of which was that Lieutenant Edwardes was made the bearer of two letters to the British General, and given his release. Umra Khan explained to him his views at great length, and under an escort he left at midnight. Taking a circuitous route to avoid a collection of ruffians in the valley, he arrived at 10 A.M. at Sadoo, the head-quarters of the British forces now advancing to the relief of Chitral. Umra Khan hoped by delivering up the British officer to stave off the punishment which the British forces were now at hand to inflict upon him. But General Low did not stay his advance for a moment. He pushed steadily on towards Umra Khan's stronghold at Munda, and on April the 16th Umra Khan played his second card, and released Lieutenant Fowler. But still General Low pressed on as will presently be described.

Both officers had now unexpectedly obtained their release. They had suffered the greatest hardships, and lived in daily peril of their lives, but they spoke with something like enthusiasm of the good treatment they had received at Umra Khan's hands. It was sometimes no easy matter for that chief to keep off those who had wished to injure the British officers; and on one occasion after Lieutenant Edwardes had left, Fowler had had an anxious time owing to the presence of many fanatics from outside striving to gain an entrance into the fort. There had nearly been a pitched fight between Umra Khan's men and these wild ruffians, and a few days afterwards when I stood with him in Umra Khan's fort, Lieutenant Fowler, standing in the doorway of the house he had occupied as a prisoner only three days before, had shown me the spot where these fanatics came clamouring round his guard, and trying to obtain access to him. But Umra Khan succeeded in protecting him throughout. He gave back to Lieutenant Edwardes his own sword which had been seized at Reshun, and which Umra Khan had received as a present from Chitral; and he promised to obtain Lieutenant Fowler's also, if it could be found. "We both consider," say the British officers, at the close of their report, "that Umra Khan treated us very well indeed, and that he never intended to be the direct cause of injury to us under any circumstance."

So ended the wonderful adventures of these two British subalterns. When they were holding out at Reshun, and making their last stand in a mere village house against overwhelming numbers of the enemy; and again, when they were treacherously captured by a deceitful foe; and lastly, when they were in the hands of men in the fever-heat of rebellion against the British, no one would have supposed that they could ever have escaped alive. But they had survived every peril, and were now once more in safety among their fellow-countrymen.

How General Low advanced to the Relief has now to be related.

CHAPTER III

GENERAL LOW'S ADVANCE

From the time that Lord Roberts made his famous march from Kabul to Kandahar, the Indian Army had hitherto taken part in no campaign so rapid, brilliant, and successful as the operations which resulted in the relief of the sorely pressed garrison of Chitral. No element was wanting to call forth the keenest instincts of the soldier, or to arouse the anxious interest of those who watched with breathless suspense the keen struggle, as the columns pushed forward over high mountain passes, girth deep in snow, across rivers broad and deep, swollen with rain and melting snow, and fiercely opposed by the desperate bravery of mountain warriors born and bred to the sword. When therefore within three short weeks the welcome news was flashed down the wire that Chitral was relieved, and that the British agent and his escort had been snatched from a horrible fate, there was perhaps hardly a corner of the British Empire which did not feel proud of the hardy leaders and brave men who had so signally upheld the proud standard of British resource, pluck, and endurance.

The general plan of operations was this. The 1st Division of all arms, some 15,000 strong, belonging to the 1st Army Corps was to mobilise at Peshawur, and moving from a southerly position as rapidly as possible, was to pass through Swat and Dir, falling on the rear of Umra Khan. At the same time a small column some 400 strong was to move from Chilas and taking the wide circuit through Gilgit and Mastuj, was to endeavour to force its way to Chitral from a north-easterly direction.

Before the opening of the campaign, our knowledge of that portion of the theatre of operations which lies between the Peshawur Valley and Chitral territory was limited almost entirely to such information as had been collated from the reports of natives. This information though defective in accuracy of detail, yet described with sufficient exactness, the main physical difficulties to be overcome. Speaking generally, the theatre of war was crossed transversely by ranges of high mountains and rapid rivers, each in itself a formidable obstacle, culminating in the lofty range through which a pass 10,450 feet high alone gave access to Chitral. Of the country which lies between Chilas and Chitral, by the route followed by Colonel Kelly's column, we had accurate knowledge, the route having been frequently traversed by troops and an accurate survey made. The stupendous task placed before Colonel Kelly, moving at this time of year, could therefore be fairly gauged beforehand.

The Lowarai Pass in May.

With the fuller knowledge we now possess it is possible to give more in detail the physical features of the country through which the Relief column of Peshawur passed. Skirting the broad open plain in which Peshawur is situated is a range of mountains varying from 3,000 feet to 6,000 feet in height, and known locally and collectively as the "border hills," for, generally speaking, the British border runs along the foot of this range. Beyond the border range lies the richly cultivated Swat Valley, varying in width from two miles to three miles, and having an extent of some thirty-six miles lengthways. Down this valley flows the Swat River, a considerable stream at all times of the year, but after the snows begin to melt, and the summer rains burst, a large and rapid river. Some estimate of the size of the river may be gained by noting that at the point first bridged by our troops, it is about half-a-mile wide from bank to bank, being split up into seven channels each requiring a separate bridge. The north side of the Swat Valley is formed by the Laram range of mountains varying from 5,000 feet to 6,000 feet in height. Beyond the Laram range we come to the southern extremity of the Principality of Dir, down the main valley of which flows the formidable and treacherous Panjkora River. This river which one day is fordable may the next be found a roaring torrent, many feet deep; indeed on one occasion it rose fourteen feet within a few hours, with little or no warning. The Panjkora Valley throughout its length is narrow, with steep rocky spurs constantly running down to the water's edge, and except in the depth of winter when the water is at its lowest, was not suitable, without extensive road making, for the passage of troops.

Lying to the east of the Panjkora Valley, and separated from it by high ranges, we find the broad, open, fertile valleys of Jandul and Bajaur, the former of these being the original home and limited territory of the chief Umra Khan, against whose power the British expedition was mainly directed. Skirting the north end of the Jandul Valley comes the Janbatai range, varying from 6,000 feet to 10,000 feet in height, crossing which we drop into a series of narrow, rocky valleys which betoken the approaches to some great mountain range. Such are the Baraul and Upper Dir Valleys, with no room for cultivation on any scale, and barely capable of supporting a miserably poor and backward race. Running transversely across the north corner of Dir territory we come to the mighty range of mountains, from 10,000 feet to 20,000 feet in height, over which the Lowarai Pass alone gives military access to the Chitral Valley. The Chitral Valley is itself very narrow and rocky, much on a par with the Panjkora Valley, and was, till a track was cut, very difficult for the passage of troops.

Briefly it may be stated that four high ranges of mountains, and three considerable rivers, besides mountain torrents, had to be crossed by the Southern column of the Relief Force.

The country through which the small Northern column under Colonel Kelly had to pass was still more rough and rugged. Moreover he was practically isolated and had to depend entirely on his own resources for those necessities which are requisite for pushing an armed force through a difficult country under the most unfavourable climatic conditions. The highest pass which was crossed by this column was over 12,000 feet, the account of the passage of which will appear when the heroic struggle of this column is dealt with in detail.

Speaking generally then, the theatre of war may be described as a mass of mountains, amidst which wind deep and rapid torrents, whilst here and there may be found small open valleys with sufficient supplies only to maintain the inhabitants.

As mentioned before, incidentally, the plan of operations for the Relief of Chitral consisted of a combined movement from north and south, the Southern column being a strong force capable of holding its own against any combination that might arise, whilst the Northern column consisted of a mere handful of men lightly equipped, whose errand it was to arrive as soon as possible, and by the moral effect of their arrival more than by actual force of arms, to prolong the siege sufficiently for the arrival of the main relief force. The Southern force was based on Nowshera (near Peshawur) whilst the Northern column was based on Gilgit.

The enemy's main base of operations was Jandul, the home of the ruling spirit in the camp of the besiegers of Chitral. Hence Umra Khan drew the pick of his men, his treasure lay here, and such arms and ammunition as he possessed were drawn from here. If we look at Jandul on the map and examine its relative position to Chitral and Peshawur we shall at once see that a decisive blow struck from the direction of Peshawur must inevitably jeopardize Umra Khan's base of operations, with the probable result that he would be compelled to leave Chitral and retreat hastily to defend his own country. The Peshawur column in fact by the nature of its march must take him directly in rear, and he must either abandon his own country to the invader in the hope of first striking a decisive blow at Chitral, afterwards turning on his tracks to meet Sir Robert Low, or else he must perforce abandon the siege and concentrate his forces to meet the British before they could gain a footing in his territory. The relative position of the belligerents being thus, it is apparent that the first objective of the main column of the Relief Force was Jandul. But though at first sight the advantage of position lay with the British, yet one important item entered into the problem which made the balance even, and that was the consideration of time. It was calculated that the Chitral garrison was only provisioned up to the end of April, and therefore to effect its relief a decisive blow must be struck before that date. Such a possibility Umra Khan and his lieutenant Sher Afzul were inclined to discountenance. An organised army moves slowly, immense physical difficulties stood in its way, and the inveterate animosity of 30,000 tribesmen could infallibly be counted upon. In a matter which depended upon days and even hours here lay a distinct advantage on the side of the besiegers.

Orders were issued for the mobilisation at Peshawur of the 1st Division of the 1st Army Corps on March 19th, the base being afterwards shifted to Nowshera as more convenient. This being the first occasion on which a serious mobilisation of any part of the army had been attempted, the experiment was watched with much interest by military critics. It must be remembered that to mobilise a force on the Indian frontier is a far more complicated and difficult problem than to mobilise a force at Metz or Strasburg. In Europe many railways lead to important points of concentration, the distances are comparatively short, and countries which are likely to become the theatre of war are intersected by numerous railways as well as roads suitable for heavy wheeled traffic. Large towns and flourishing villages are to be found at the end of every march, and the country invaded is capable of supplying to a very great extent the wants of the invaders in the matter of commissariat and transport. Far differently situated is a force on the Indian frontier destined to penetrate into the inhospitable mountains which frown along its whole length from the Bay of Bengal to the deserts of Beluchistan. For such a force in addition to food for the men, nearly all the grain, and much even of the hay for the animals, has to be carried up to the most advanced troops from the base in India, and carried not along macadamised roads in capacious carts, but by mountain paths where pack transport is alone possible.

There is a popular error that the impedimenta of an Indian Division is enormous; indeed, it has been gravely stated by a serious military critic that it is no uncommon thing for regiments in India to take their mahogany mess tables on service with them. Of course only ignorance of the country and its ways, with a hazy recollection of Chillianwallah and the historic mess table of the 24th Foot, could be responsible for such an erroneous statement. As a matter of fact during this campaign the allowance per man for everything was 10 lbs., and per officer 40 lbs., and no tents were allowed. When we consider that an ordinary soldier's blanket weighs 4 or 5 lbs., an allowance of 10 lbs. need not be called extravagant in a country where snow and ice, heavy rain, and the fiery heat of the sun had in turns to be encountered. Yet marching thus light 28,000 pack animals had to be collected to feed and maintain the force. It will be apparent, then, that the problem of mobilisation on the Indian frontier is very materially complicated by the conditions that exist. Not only the troops and their stores have to be concentrated, but also many thousands of pack animals, and the food for the entire force, man and beast, for as long as the campaign lasts. Add to this that units had in some cases to come immense distances, that the line of railway was a single one, and that the detraining station was a small roadside station without platforms, or conveniences, for disembarking troops, animals, and stores, and we have a compendium of difficulties which would try severely the most perfectly organised scheme of mobilisation.

It was therefore a source of gratification to the military authorities that the scheme and the railway stood so well the severe test applied to them. On the 1st of April the Division, fully equipped and provisioned, made the first march of the campaign. The force consisted of three Infantry Brigades, each of four regiments, two of which were British and two native; the Divisional troops consisted of two regiments of cavalry, four batteries of Mountain Artillery, one[1] regiment of Pioneers, and three[2] companies of Sappers and Miners. In addition, three regiments of infantry were told off as lines of communication troops. The command of the force was given to Lieutenant-General Sir Robert Low, K.C.B., with Brigadier-General Bindon Blood, C.B., Royal Engineers, as his chief staff officer. The three brigades were commanded by Brigadier-Generals A. A. Kinloch, C.B., H. G. Waterfield, and W. F. Gatacre, D.S.O.; whilst the lines of communication were entrusted to Brigadier-General A. G. Hammond, V.C., C.B., D.S.O., A.D.C.

[1] Afterwards increased.

[2] Afterwards increased.

The column under Colonel Kelly will be dealt with separately in a later chapter.

CHAPTER IV

ACTIONS AT THE MALAKAND AND PANJKORA

If we look at the map of the country we shall see that the frontier at this point is crossed by three main passes, all leading into the Swat Valley. These passes, in order from east to west, are the Mora Pass, the Shahkot Pass, and the Malakand Pass. All were reported equally difficult and each about 3,500 feet high, with a rough footpath, possible for laden animals, leading over each. From reasons of policy it was decided not to use the Mora Pass, with the idea of not disturbing unnecessarily possibly hostile tribes on that flank. There remained the Shahkot and Malakand Passes. A proclamation was sent on in advance to the people of Swat, saying that the British Government had no hostile intentions against them, but merely asked for right of way through their territory; such a concession being liberally paid for. Had the people of Swat elected to accept these pacific terms a simultaneous advance would have been made by both passes; but intelligence was received that all the passes were strongly held, and especially so the Shahkot Pass. Sir Robert Low therefore decided to merely threaten the Shahkot and Mora Passes, whilst his real attack was made on the Malakand Pass. With this plan in view the 1st Brigade bivouacked at Lundkwar in full sight of, and directly threatening, the Shahkot Pass; whilst a strong cavalry reconnaissance was made towards the Mora Pass to stir up dust and to distract the enemy's attention from the true point of attack. The passes are, roughly speaking, about seven miles apart, and as soon as it was found that the enemy was irrevocably committed to defend all those passes, Sir Robert Low issued orders to concentrate on his left, and with his whole force stormed the Malakand Pass.

The battle took place on April 3rd, on the very day that Colonel Kelly's column crossed the Shandur Pass far away to the north, the 2nd Brigade under Brigadier-General Waterfield leading, supported by the 1st Brigade under Brigadier-General Kinloch, whilst the 3rd Brigade under Brigadier-General Gatacre was held in reserve. The enemy's position extended along the crest of the pass, holding the heights on either flank, whilst a series of breastworks built of stone, each commanding the one below, were pushed down the main spurs. The position was of extraordinary strength, and one which in the hands of an organised enemy would have taken a week to capture. The enemy's numbers were afterwards found to be about 12,000, about half of whom were armed, whilst the remainder were occupied in carrying off the killed and wounded, fetching water, and bowling down huge rocks on the assaulting columns. The extent of the position may be put down at one and a half miles. The regiments chiefly engaged were the King's Own Scottish Borderers, the Gordon Highlanders, the Guides, and the 4th Sikhs, all of the 2nd Brigade; and the Bedfordshire Regiment, the 60th Rifles, the 15th Sikhs, and the 37th Dogras composing the 1st Brigade. Three mountain batteries massed under Major Dacres Cunningham also took a conspicuous part in the fight, whilst three Maxim guns also did their share towards defeating the enemy.

The plan of attack was as follows. The Guides supported later by the 4th Sikhs, were to scale the precipitous height on the extreme right of the enemy's position, then turning inwards the two regiments were to sweep along the crest, taking the enemy in flank whilst the frontal attack was pushed home. It was calculated that the Guides would take three hours to reach the crest, but so stern was the resistance, and so jagged and perpendicular the ascent, that it took these practised mountaineers five hours before they had captured the last sangar and crowned the heights. Meanwhile as the day was drawing on it was considered inadvisable to delay longer the frontal attack, for the enemy had been now under a most searching and accurate shell fire from three batteries for the space of upwards of three hours and were naturally much shaken by it, whilst the action of the Guides had made itself well felt on his right flank; orders were therefore given for the King's Own Scottish Borderers and the Gordon Highlanders to advance to the attack, each being directed up a separate spur.

It was a fine and stirring sight to see the splendid dash with which the two Scotch regiments took the hill. From valley to crest at this point the height varies from 1,000 to 1,500 feet and the slope looks for the most part almost perpendicular. It was this very steepness which partly accounted for the comparatively small loss suffered from the enemy's fire and the showers of huge boulders which were hurled upon the assailants; but the chief reason for this happy immunity was the wonderfully spirited manner in which the men rushed breastwork after breastwork, and arrived just beneath the final ridge before the enemy had time to realise that the assaulting columns were at their very feet.

When the whole of the 2nd Brigade had thus got well under way orders were given for the 1st Brigade to support them, the 60th Rifles, followed by the 15th Sikhs, being sent up a re-entrant, which intervened between the King's Own Scottish Borderers and the Guides, whilst the Bedfordshire Regiment and 37th Dogras, heading on up the valley passed across the front of the enemy's position, and, circling round the rear of the Gordon Highlanders, attacked the enemy's extreme left, overlapping it considerably. The 60th Rifles after ascending some way suddenly came across an old Buddhist road, and turning sharp to their right along this soon found themselves level with the leading companies of the King's Own Scottish Borderers. The whole line now took a moment's breathing time, to collect the men still struggling up in small groups, and to get into wind for the final rush. As soon as all was ready bayonets were fixed, the bugle's cheery call to advance was sounded, and with a great shout the position which from below appears almost impregnable was carried at the point of the bayonet; the three British regiments reaching the crest at almost the same moment. Meanwhile the Guides and 4th Sikhs had stormed the lofty peak away on our left, and were ready to move inwards if such support had been necessary; whilst the Bedfordshire Regiment and 37th Dogras scaling the heights before them dashed down the far valley in hot pursuit of the enemy, only halting when they reached the large walled village of Khar on the Swat River.

The Malakand Pass.

Thus brilliantly was an exceptionally strong position carried, and the first obstacle which lay in the path of the Southern column of the Relief Force brushed away. The action lasted five hours, and it is difficult to praise too highly the dash and determination with which the pass was carried. Nor is it possible to forget the sterling bravery of the enemy, who for five hours withstood a most searching and splendidly-directed shell fire from three batteries, and yet were still firm enough to stand up to a bayonet charge at the end of it. Their loss was computed by themselves at 500 killed, and the general average of battles would make their wounded probably reach a total of 1,000, or, say, a total loss of from 1,250 to 1,500. The British loss was under seventy killed and wounded.

Several curious cases of the vitality of the wounded was furnished by both sides. A man of the Guides, hit in the region of the stomach, climbed down to the foot of the pass, and walked five miles back to the Field Hospital, supported by a comrade. One of the enemy on the other hand, with no less than six bullets through him, walked all the way to Chakdara, nine miles off, and was afterwards treated by our surgeons, and, strange to say, made a rapid recovery. There is no doubt that Asiatics can stand wounds inflicted by sword or bullet infinitely better than Europeans can. Wounds that would kill a European, or at any rate lay him up for months, affect these hardy and abstemious mountaineers in a very much less severe manner. Imagine, for instance, having the whole lock of an exploded gun blown into one's shoulder, and going about as if nothing in particular had happened! Yet such a lock was cut out of a man's shoulder months after the occurrence by one of our surgeons. Marvellous cases of recovery, without number, might be told, but perhaps the case of quite a young boy is as typical as any. Like boys in any other part of the world, hearing that a fight was going to take place hard by, he naturally determined to go and look on. Whilst he was thoroughly enjoying himself in all the excitement of the fight, and probably throwing stones vigorously, a stray bullet hit him in the arm, passing through it in several places and splintering it badly. When the pass was taken he was found lying wounded, and his wound was examined. The doctors decided that he must have his arm cut off, or mortification would certainly set in, and they gave the boy the choice between death or the amputation of his arm. He chose the former, but in a few days instead of being dead he was better, and in a few days more was out and about again.

Concealed amongst the rocks, boulders, and bushes, the enemy formed a most difficult mark to hit; whilst the same causes, combined with the steepness of the ground, saved our troops from severer loss. The admirable control under which our infantry fire was kept may be gauged by the fact that the average expenditure of ammunition was under seven rounds per man throughout the day.

Of the enemy's bravery it is difficult to speak too highly, and individual cases were conspicuous. One leader, carrying a large red and white banner, called on his men to charge the Scottish Borderers when they were half way up the hill. The charge was made, but all his followers gradually fell, till the leader alone was left. Nothing daunted he held steadily on, now and again falling, heavily hit, but up and on again without a moment's delay, till at last he was shot dead close to the British line. More desperate courage than this is difficult to imagine. Again, one of the enemy's drummers, not content with taking his fair share of risks, persisted in mounting on to the roof of a hut, where he showed up clear and conspicuous against the sky line, and thence cheered on his comrades. Every now and again a bullet would find him out, and he would drop to dress his wounds, and then again mounting recommenced beating his drum. At last a bullet got him through the heart, and he fell headlong a hundred yards down the cliff, and there lay stark dead, but with his drum round his neck, and his arms ready raised to strike it. No doubt the great Mahomed will find a place for him in the ranks of the Mussulman Paradise.

On the night after the battle, the crest of the pass was held by the 1st Brigade, with two regiments pushed down as far as Khar, whilst the 2nd Brigade bivouacked at the south entrance of the pass. On the following morning commenced the stupendous task of pushing over the pass the ammunition, baggage, and supplies of the advanced brigades. The only available path was a single track very steep and much encumbered with boulders, which had been hastily improved by working parties of Sappers and Pioneers. Up this, from dawn to dusk, toiled batch after batch of laden mules, and yet at the end of the day small progress had been made. At this highly opportune moment it was discovered that the old Buddhist road, hit off by the 60th Rifles during the assault, led down by a good gradient to the plains. Every available man was immediately employed in improving this relic of a civilisation 2,000 years old, with the result that in another twenty-four hours the brigades were ready to move. Had it not been for this Buddhist road, the very existence of which appeared to have been forgotten by the present inhabitants, it would have taken many days to get the division across the Malakand Pass.

Whilst the work on the pass was going on, the 1st Brigade moved down into the Swat Valley, and was fiercely assailed by several thousand of the enemy, who, finding the Shahkot and Mora Passes turned, came streaming westward, determined on a fight. These large bodies of men appeared on the spurs which flanked the advance of the 1st Brigade, and it became necessary to hold them in check till the brigade with its baggage could get clear into the open valley. This duty was successfully performed by the 37th Dogras, who crowned a neighbouring spur, as well as by the Mountain Artillery, which kept the enemy's crest well swept. Towards evening, however, the enemy, mistaking the defensive attitude of our troops, who were merely covering the advance of the remainder, were reported to be boldly issuing into the plain to the number of 2,000, making as if to sweep round the foot of the spur where it meets the plain, with a view to charging on to the head and flank of the advancing column. Receiving warning of this movement, orders were immediately given for the mere handful of cavalry which had been able so far to struggle over the pass to trot round the spur, and to watch for a chance of falling on the enemy in the open. This small body consisted of fifty sabres of the Guides Cavalry under Captain R. B. Adams and Lieutenant G. M. Baldwin, who, on reconnoitring round the spur, found the enemy in the open, but, like all mountaineers, hugging the foothills. Seeing his chance, Captain Adams, with great promptness and boldness, charged, doing great execution, and driving the whole mass of the enemy headlong into the hills. Not only was the charge brilliant and effective, but the moral effect was enormous. The enemy had not the remotest notion that any cavalry had crossed the pass, and like all nations unaccustomed to horses, they had exaggerated notions of the power of cavalry. When, therefore, they saw their worst fears more than realised, and fifty sabres without a moment's hesitation charging a couple of thousand foot soldiers and completely altering the aspect of the fight, the ascendency of the cavalry arm was established for the campaign. Even Fowler and Edwardes, in their far-off captivity, heard nothing reiterated so much as this dread of cavalry. The immediate result was that the enemy began to melt away even from the hill tops, and by next morning not a vestige of them was to be seen. Our losses on this day were slight, including seven or eight in the cavalry, whilst the enemy suffered severely, at least 250 being killed.

On the 5th and 6th of April, reconnaissances under the Chief Staff Officer, General Blood, were pushed up the valley to search for fords across the Swat River, and to keep in touch with the enemy, who could be seen in considerable force beyond Thana. Suitable points of passage having been found, the duty of forcing the passage was entrusted to General Waterfield and the 2nd Brigade. The enemy now left Thana and crossing the river were reinforced by a body of riflemen sent down by Umra Khan under the command of his brother. In all about 4,500 men were posted in a naturally strong position to oppose the passage of the British force. On the enemy's bank small rocky hills at the water's edge, completely commanded the perfectly level and open southern bank, from which the attack had to be delivered. Naturally a frontal attack would have been very costly, but General Waterfield's smart tactical instinct showed him the way to gain his end with but slight loss. Engaging the enemy heavily at long ranges with his artillery and the main body of his Infantry, he sent the Guides Cavalry and 11th Bengal Lancers up the river with orders to cross by a little-known ford, and to fall briskly on the flank and rear of the enemy. To support the cavalry he sent the 15th Sikh Infantry. The effect was instantaneous; the defenders of the passage the moment they saw the dreaded Lancers, half swimming, half wading, across the river, a mile or so up stream, began to lose heart; and what at first was a retirement gradually degenerated into a flight, headed by Umra Khan's brother and the body of horsemen escorting him. But the Lancers and Guides were not to be denied, and falling on the demoralised foe, left the green crops strewn with their dead. The enemy's total loss was about 400 killed, of whom about one hundred fell to the cavalry. Holding the north bank with two battalions, fords were rapidly marked out, and the infantry, aided by inflated skins, and the skilled watermen of the country impressed for the service, struggled across with only two or three casualties from drowning. The work was an anxious one, for armpit deep in the rushing torrent a man washed off his legs was lost for ever.

During the cavalry pursuit one of the squadrons of the 11th Bengal Lancers narrowly missed capturing Umra Khan's brother, which at the time would have been a great *coup*. For it must be remembered that two British officers, Lieutenants Edwardes and Fowler, were all this time prisoners in Umra Khan's hands, and entirely at his mercy. It may be said that the halter was round their necks, and every blow our forces struck served but to tighten the knot. With Umra Khan's brother in our hands the situation would have been reciprocated, and we could then have afforded to treat on equal terms for an exchange. During this same pursuit a curious incident occurred. One or two of the enemy made a stand close to a tree in the plain; at them charged a trooper, lance well down, as hard as he could gallop; whether he hit his man or not history does not relate, but the next second he found himself and his horse at the bottom of a well, which without side walls stood behind the tree. His horse was killed, but he himself escaped with a bad shaking. If one may hark so far back a similar accident met an uncle of the author's, Lieutenant George Younghusband, of the 5th Punjab Cavalry, in the Mutiny. He was charging with his squadron with Greathead's column, on their march to the relief of Agra, when he came across a blind well, down which he fell, with his mounted orderly on top of him. His orderly and the two horses were killed, and he alone came out alive, but alas! only to be killed in another charge shortly afterwards.

In the village of Chakdara, which lies near the main ford on the north bank, many arms were found, and amongst others a straight officer's sword, cavalry pattern, by Wilkinson, of London. As the number was on the sword, application was made to Messrs. Wilkinson to find out from their books the name of the original owner of the sword. It turned out to be an officer of the name of Bellew. This proved to be Lieutenant Bellew of the 10th Hussars, who served in Afghanistan in 1878-79, with his regiment. This sword he had lent to Lieutenant Harford, who was drowned with a troop of the 10th Hussars in the Kabul River. We had here evidence of the immense strength of the class of stone fort built by Umra Khan. The fort is called Ramora, and lay east of Chakdara, being Umra Khan's advanced fort, with which he practically dominated the entire Swat Valley. This was captured after a short resistance, and sentenced to be blown up by the Sappers. But sentence was one thing, and execution another. A heavy charge was placed at the foot of one of the towers, the train lighted, and the spectators stood afar off, expecting to see the whole structure lifted sky high. There was a very loud report indeed, but that was all, for the tower stood perfectly unmoved. On further examination it was found that the base of each tower was perfectly solid masonry from the foundation to fifteen feet above ground line, whilst the walls above were of immense thickness. All the forts built by Umra Khan were of the same pattern, that is, four-cornered, with one of these strong towers at each corner, and with high walls of great thickness and carefully loopholed forming the four sides. Our artillery could make no impression on these forts. The sites chosen in the open valleys are very good; but in the narrow valleys they are perforce much commanded by the neighbouring precipitous hills. On the Swat River, the enemy's position, with the fort of Ramora on one flank, rocky hills well prepared for defence on the other, the village of Chakdara in the centre, with much swampy ground restricting the advance of an enemy even after the passage of the river to a few well-defined paths, combined to make the position if scientifically held a remarkably strong one.

Directly the passage of the Swat River had been effected the Sappers were set to work to construct a trestle and pier bridge, whilst strong reconnaissances were sent forward to keep in touch with the enemy. These found the Katgola Pass over the Laram Range unoccupied, and the cavalry pushing on descended on to the

Panjkora River, some twenty miles ahead. Here was found the most formidable obstacle which the force had yet encountered. On April 9th, the river was fordable for horses and, with difficulty, also for infantry; on the 11th, it was barely fordable for horses, and not at all for Infantry; but from that time onwards it became a mighty torrent totally unfordable, impracticable also for cavalry swimming, though the Indian trooper and his horse are like ducks in the water. It became necessary therefore to build a bridge.

The only materials immediately at hand were the heavy logs of wood, parts of great trees which are annually floated down from these regions to India, for sale. With these, and using telegraph wire to anchor the piers, a rough footbridge was with great difficulty and danger constructed, and floated into position. On the night of April 12th, the Guides were pushed across, and strongly entrenched, so as to cover the bridge head. The night passed quietly, but towards morning a freshet came down bearing great logs and washed the bridge away, leaving the Guides on the far side. The position was undoubtedly an awkward one, for cavalry reconnaissances had reported that the enemy in some strength, calculated at 9,000 by the local people, lay only about seven miles westward, and the news of the bridge breaking would immediately be reported by their outlooks. However it never does in fighting these people to hesitate or appear to be in the least discomposed, happen what may. Colonel Battye, who was commanding the Guides on this occasion, therefore adhered to the orders received overnight, when the bridge was intact. These orders were to turn the enemy's sharpshooters out of the positions from which they had been annoying our working parties, and to burn such villages near at hand as had been furnishing armed parties to fire across the river by night and day. The bold offensive thus taken by the Guides undoubtedly had a good effect. They started early in the morning, and making a wide sweep drove out all parties of the enemy concealed amongst the rocks, and burnt such villages as were actively hostile. All this was easy work for troops highly skilled in hill warfare, though the climbing was very stiff; but the really stern trial came when the hour arrived to retire to the bridge head. It requires the very best and steadiest of troops to carry out a retirement in the face of great odds, and it requires still greater nerve to do so in the presence of brave and fanatical foes who count life as nothing, who with matchless courage charge right up to the muzzle of a breech-loader, and who give no quarter and ask for none.

In retiring before such an enemy an almost exaggerated deliberation is required, for the least appearance of hurry, much more so of confusion, will open the sluice gates and let in such a stormy torrent of warriors, that science must perforce give way to weight of numbers.

The story of the day's fighting may thus be briefly told. The Guides had completed their mission on which they had been despatched, and were now retiring down the spurs of a lofty hill which forms the angle where the Jandul River flows into the Panjkora River. This hill is to the south of the Jandul River, whilst the bridge head was to the north of it. Thus, to reach their entrenched position the Guides had to retire down the mountain they were on and to cross the Jandul River. At about noon two dense columns of the enemy were seen coming down the

Jandul Valley, one column keeping to the right bank, and the other to the left bank of the Jandul River. The first column, breasting the mountain out of range of the Guides and mostly hidden from them by an intervening spur, reached the summit and attacked the regiment strongly as it retired. The second column sweeping down the valley prepared to assail the Guides in flank and rear, hoping to completely cut off their retreat. Foot by foot—to the spectators it seemed almost inch by inch—the different companies retired alternately down the ridges they occupied, fiercely assailed on all hands yet coolly firing volley after volley, relinquishing quietly and almost imperceptibly one strong position only to take up another a few yards back, the splendidly-directed fire of the Derajat Mountain Battery doing invaluable service. So good indeed was the fire discipline of the troops engaged under these trying circumstances that not a shot was fired except by word of command. Meanwhile two companies of the regiment, which had been left to hold the bridge head, moved out to check the advance of the enemy's second column, which, making a detour, was moving with determination into the flank and rear of the retreating force. The whole of the 2nd Brigade, a battery of artillery, and a Maxim gun, were now ordered out and placed in a strong position on the east bank of the Panjkora (the Guides being on the west bank), whence in the later stages of the retirement their fire could be of material assistance. Owing to the very broken nature of the mountain sides, and the excellent cover afforded to skilled skirmishers, our loss was exceedingly small till the foot of the hill was reached. Here the regiment had to cross several hundred yards of level ground, on which the green barley was standing waist high, and then cross the Jandul River, here about three feet deep, to make its way through more fields to the bridge head. Unhappily, just as the regiment left the last spur, the commanding officer, Lieutenant-Colonel F. D. Battye was mortally wounded, dying, as he would perhaps most wish to, at the head of his regiment, after a quarter of a century of distinguished service with it.

It was in crossing this open ground that the extraordinary bravery of the enemy became more brilliantly evident. Standard-bearers with reckless gallantry could be seen rushing to certain destruction, falling perhaps within ten yards of the invincible line of the Guides. Nay, sometimes men, devoid of all fear, and having used up the whole of their ammunition, rushed forward with large rocks and hurled these at the soldiers, courting instant death. They were like hounds on their prey. Nothing could damp their ardour or check the fury of their assaults. Even after the Guides had crossed the Jandul stream, and the enemy were under a severe flank fire from the Gordon Highlanders and the King's Own Scottish Borderers, they dashed into the stream, where each one stood out as clear as a bull's eye on a target, and attempted to close again. But not a man got across, so steady and well directed was the flank fire of the British regiments. The fight was now practically over for the day; fire slackened all round, and the entrenched position was rapidly occupied, and strengthened where necessary. During the day the enemy, who numbered 5,000, lost from 500 to 600 men; the Guides' total loss was only about twenty, a result due to the skilful manner in which the retirement was effected, as well as to the fine cover afforded by the broken ground on the mountain side.

Constructing a Suspension Bridge over the Panjkora River.

It was now evening, and preparations had to be made to meet a night attack, for the enemy, several thousand strong, were still close round hidden behind the low hills. As a reinforcement a couple of companies of the 4th Sikhs and some extra British officers were sent across on rafts, also a Maxim gun; whilst the near bank, which commanded the bridge head entrenchment at 800 yards' range, was occupied by a mountain battery, and the troops of the 2nd Brigade. The position of the enemy being such as it was, the night was one of some anxiety, for a determined rush might be expected at any moment. Such an attack was planned and on the eve of being executed, when the unexpected, and as it seemed to the enemy, magical, appearance of a star shell completely dumfounded the hitherto dauntless foe, and the attack was not delivered. From the information of spies it appeared afterwards that 2,000 chosen warriors, sword in hand, lay concealed in the standing corn just outside the picquets, merely awaiting the signal for assault, when this happy contrivance of civilisation staved off a fight, which could only have been attended with enormous loss on both sides. Before the enemy finally drew off, however, the force sustained a serious loss in the death of Captain Peebles, in charge of the Maxim gun. This officer's services had proved invaluable from his intimate knowledge of the working of the Maxim, a gun which in inexpert hands is apt, like other pieces of mechanism, to get out of order. The working of Captain Peebles's gun had been the admiration of the whole force throughout the campaign.

It had become sufficiently apparent now that no floating bridge could hope to stand the current in the Panjkora River, and it was therefore decided to throw across a suspension bridge at a point somewhat lower down. Curiously enough at this point, where the rocky hills shut in the river till it is like a mill race only 100 feet or so across, were found bridging materials collected by Umra Khan, who had evidently ordered a cantilever bridge to be built here. The work was entrusted to Major Aylmer, V.C., R.E., who had had much experience in this branch of his art up in the Gilgit direction. The available materials were telegraph wire and beams from dismantled houses. With these, within forty-eight hours, Major Aylmer constructed a suspension bridge of 100 feet span, capable of bearing even loaded camels, cavalry, and mountain artillery.

During the construction a very prompt and plucky act on Major Aylmer's part saved the life of a soldier. About a mile up stream, where the first floating bridge had been constructed, a flying bridge and rafts were still working backwards and forwards, to supply the Guides with their wants on the other bank. One of these rafts, on which were two men of the Devonshire Regiment Maxim Gun Detachment, got accidentally overturned, and the boatmen and oars were washed away. The two soldiers managed to climb on to the raft and were carried down stream at a great pace. General Gatacre, seeing the accident, immediately galloped down to the site of the new bridge to give warning, in the hopes of saving the men. Meanwhile one man had made an attempt to jump on shore, and had been swept away and drowned, and the survivor on the raft came flying down the torrent. With the greatest presence of mind and pluck Major Aylmer immediately slipped down a slack wire that was across the river, and just managed to grab the soldier as he shot past. The raft was immediately after dashed to pieces on the rocks below.

With considerable difficulty the soldier and his preserver were hauled on shore, and it was then found that the Major was badly bruised and cut by the wire. The Royal Humane Society's medal has been given for many a less distinguished act of bravery, yet I do not think that in the stir of passing events it actually occurred to any of the spectators to send the recommendation home.

Certain news came in about now that Lieutenants Edwardes and Fowler, the two officers who had fallen into Umra Khan's hands, were at Barwa, a small fort only about eighteen miles distant, on the other side of the Panjkora. This rather complicated matters, for according to all precedent and our former experiences of Pathan warfare these officers' lives were not worth an hour's purchase in any case, and their murder in cold blood might be calculated on as a moral certainty if we were to attack. The following note was received from the officers, written from Barwa:—"Fowler R.E. and Edwardes 2nd Bombay Grenadiers are shut in Barwa can you get us out. Give bearers Rs.100. 7.4.94 (*sic*) P.S. Shall we try and bolt people here panic." A hasty scrawl written on the leaf of a note-book.

The title "Political" officers is one of ill omen in the Indian Army, but in Major Deane the force had a guide, philosopher, and friend whose services throughout were simply invaluable. Added to an intimate knowledge of the country, its people, and language, he added a shrewd knowledge of how to deal with them. To Major Deane's diplomatic skill Lieutenants Fowler and Edwardes in all human probability owe their lives, and their release freed the General's arm to strike, unhampered by the thought that his action might sound the death-knell of the two young officers. In meeting Major Deane half way in these diplomatic overtures Umra Khan displayed an enlightened and civilised advancement which is far ahead of his surroundings. Without demanding any *quid pro quo,* he, when they were asked for, returned the prisoners in all honour, having treated them thoroughly well throughout.

Whilst the Sappers are busy building their bridge over the Panjkora this would be a not altogether unfavourable moment to epitomise the campaign in so far as it had conduced to the relief of the beleaguered garrison up to this date. Every effort had failed to get news from the besieged, nor had it been found possible by any device—for many were tried—to throw news of the coming succour into the fort. But so far great results had been gained; the commander-in-chief, the soul and body of the siege, Umra Khan himself, with one thousand of his picked men, mostly armed with breech-loaders, had been compelled to abandon the siege, and to hasten back southwards and to organise resistance to and raise the tribes against our advance. On this same date, April 13th, Colonel Kelly and his handful of men were at Mastuj, having accomplished their celebrated passage of the Shandur Pass. His advance so far had been but slightly opposed. From reliable information it was supposed that the garrison of Chitral had supplies to last them only up to April 22nd. A week therefore only remained, and before the Southern force lay Umra Khan with 9,000 men and two mighty ranges of mountains, whilst the Northern force, under Colonel Kelly, though within sixty miles of Chitral, had before it a narrow and difficult route, at any point in which the enemy might be found strongly posted.

CHAPTER V

THE RELIEF OF CHITRAL

Truly on this thirteenth of April the outlook was not a bright one; but here came in one of those flashes of genius which go to win campaigns and undoubtedly helped to win this one. It occurred to those responsible for the conduct of the campaign that though it was impossible to convey a large force to Chitral in the given time, yet it was quite feasible to push through a small number of men who, falling on the rear of Sher Afzul, the general left by Umra Khan in charge of the siege, might form a welcome diversion. At first it was contemplated sending a mixed force of regulars and levies, but after careful deliberation it was decided that regulars would impede the rate of march, and that the effect being chiefly a moral one could be almost as surely gained by levies alone. The plan therefore was for the main force to cross the Panjkora, and to fight a decisive battle with Umra Khan, whilst our ally the Khan of Dir, covered by this movement, was despatched up the left bank of the Panjkora River, with orders to cross the Lowarai Pass, 10,450 feet high, to descend into the Chitral Valley, and to give out far and wide that he was merely the advanced guard of the force, which had conquered Swat and Bajour, and had heavily defeated the hitherto invincible general Umra Khan.

In pursuance of this plan the Khan of Dir was ordered to move forward with 1,000 men and to cross the Lowarai Pass, and immediately the bridge over the Panjkora River was completed, General Blood moved rapidly forward in charge of a cavalry reconnaissance towards Umra Khan's stronghold at Munda. Advancing with a squadron of the Guides Cavalry, General Blood moved up the Jandul River till the large and important village of Miankila was in sight. Here a peasant was met who entered freely into conversation. The General asked him where Umra Khan was. He said, "Over there in that fort," pointing to Munda, just over the brow of a rise in the ground. "Will you take him a note and bring an answer?" asked the General. "Certainly," said the peasant, "I will be back in half an hour." So calling to his assistance the linguistic proficiency of Captain Nixon, of the Intelligence Department, a polite and cordial note was written to Umra Khan, asking him to come out into the open and have a talk with the General, in all good fellowship, and "without prejudice." The answer came back before long, and was to the following effect: "After greetings, I should greatly like to meet your excellency, and to have a quiet talk with you, whereby the whole affair might be easily settled. But unfortunately I am surrounded by about 3,000 Ghazis, and these bad men will not hear of my going out to see. You too I notice are accompanied by warriors. Assuredly no quiet conversation can take place under these circumstances. Now I propose that you send away your army and I will send away mine, and then you and I can have our conference alone in the field." This was all very nice and friendly; but meanwhile dense columns of the enemy began to issue from Miankila and Munda, and moving with astonishing rapidity, occupied both banks of the river, which is here easily fordable everywhere, and began to press on the cavalry. The reconnoitring party moved back quietly, till the head of the infantry column became visible, hastening up. This was the 3rd Infantry Brigade under General Gatacre, accompanied by the 11th Bengal Lancers and the Derajat Mountain Battery.

The battery opened fire at once, and the cavalry moved up the river bed, here very broad and open, whilst the infantry advanced to the attack up the right bank of the stream. But from the first moment, though Umra Khan was present in person, it was quite evident that the enemy did not mean "business." The severe lessons of former battles had begun to tell upon them, and their resistance was only half-hearted. The 3rd Brigade pushed home their advantage, and the enemy retired before them, losing only a few men, till towards evening their whole force was to be seen in full retreat up the distant valley into Nawagai. The troops bivouacked in the forward position they had gained, and the 2nd Brigade was ordered up in the expectation that the enemy would make a determined stand on the morrow. But the morrow showed nothing but deserted positions and deserted forts, and thus easily had been fought and won the final engagement which decided the campaign, and sent Umra Khan, the victor in a hundred fights, ruined and broken to exile, and premature death in Kabul.

When we say ruined, however, let us understand the word in a moral sense. Pecuniarily Umra Khan is anything but ruined, for one of our spies counted eleven mule loads of treasure leaving Munda fort one night under a strong escort. Each mule would carry Rs.6,000 in silver, or Rs.120,000 in gold, or any sum one likes to mention in jewels. Taking a rough average between silver and gold, and leaving jewels out of consideration, we shall be able to calculate that eleven mule loads of treasure would keep Umra Khan and his family very comfortably for the rest of their days.

Some weeks after, when escorting Sher Afzul to India, I heard many stories of Umra Khan. Like a wise man, knowing the uncertain tenor of an Eastern monarch's reign, he had taken care to feather his nest whilst his power lasted. He exacted a tithe of their profits from all, merchants or agriculturists, and the money thus accumulated, he changed into gold at a rate of exchange fixed by himself. Thus if the real value of a Russian gold coin was Rs.20, by royal edict, and for the benefit of the royal purchaser, it became Rs.18. Gold is very scarce in Asia, but a certain number of Russian coins filter across, and gold ornaments are to be found here and there. All these Umra Khan assiduously collected, so that at the time of his flight he probably had a goodly treasure.

Dir Fort.

One evening before the British advance began, after attending evening prayers on the praying platform in the clump of chenars below Munda fort, Umra Khan, turning to his followers, said: "I have just received a letter from Gholam Hyder, the Commander-in-Chief of the Afghan army. His proposal is that I shall invade the Peshawur Valley by way of the Malakand with 30,000 men, and that he will co-operate through the Khyber Pass with 10,000 men. What say you, my brave warriors?" Whereupon the whole assembly arose with a mighty shout, "To Peshawur!" travestying a somewhat more celebrated cry which was heard in Europe in 1870. Whether such a letter had been received or not, and whether, if it had been, it was anything more than one of those neighbourly acts by which, in the East, one friend lures another to certain destruction, it is not necessary here to discuss. The anecdote is merely told as showing the immense confidence Umra Khan had in his own powers, and the faith his followers had in his skill. Years of conquest, and years of unchequered success, had led the petty border chieftain into half thinking that he could withstand the power of a mighty empire. It was a thousand pities that this chief took up the attitude he did. If he had chosen to be the friend of the British, he might now be despotic ruler of all the country which lies between Chitral and Peshawur Valley, with the firm alliance of the British Government at his back.

When the cavalry, riding on rapidly, captured the abandoned fort of Munda, every trace of a rapid flight was apparent. Books and grain were strewn about, dismounted cannon lay at the gate, everything was topsy-turvey and turned inside out, and the sole occupant was a poor, deformed idiot. Amongst the papers found lying about were some of considerable interest. One was from a certain *mullah*[3] who, before the battle, wrote from the summit of the Malakand Pass. He said: "We see the infidels, the sons of pigs, encamped down in the plains below us. There are very few of them, and we shall easily send them all to Hell. On our side we have twelve or fifteen thousand Ghazis, and the place is well fortified with sangars. To-morrow or next day I shall have the honour of informing your Excellency that the infidels have been extirpated"; and so on. It is highly probable that the worthy *mullah* spent the next few days in breaking the record towards Upper Swat, or else, perchance, his bones now lie on the Malakand.

Another literary curiosity found in Munda fort was a letter from a Scotch firm in Bombay offering to provide Umra Khan with every luxury in the way of arms and ammunition, from Maxim guns at Rs.3,700 each, down to revolvers at Rs.34 a piece. Luckily the benevolent intentions of this patriotic firm had been frustrated by the astute intervention of Major Deane, at that time Deputy Commissioner of Peshawur. The firm in question has found it expedient to transfer itself, and the benefits to humanity which it provides, to Cairo. Many other letters too lay about showing how wide was the influence of the departed chief; offers of help, spontaneous and otherwise, showed that the total resources at his command were not much under 30,000 men, all armed in some fashion or another, with a good sprinkling of breech-loading rifles, lately the property of Her Majesty the Queen of England.

---

[3] A priest, often of the sporting-parson type of Joshua of old.

Head-quarter Camp, Dir.

It was on the 17th day of April that Umra Khan made his last stand and disappeared permanently from the theatre of operations. On the very same day the garrison of Chitral made the splendid sortie led by Lieutenant Harley of the 14th Sikhs, a full account of which will appear in a future chapter, and on the night of the 18th of April the siege was raised, and Sher Afzul and his whole force fled to the hills. Here the general with 1,500 of his men, were cleverly captured and brought in prisoners to Dir.

The history of our recent wars does not furnish an example of a more signal and sweeping success. In the space of exactly one month from the day on which the mobilisation of the Relief Force was ordered, the main object of the campaign was obtained, the whole of the enemy's numerous and ubiquitous forces were defeated and dispersed, and every one of the important chiefs was a prisoner in our hands, or in those of our ally the Amir. Setting aside the superiority in armament and organisation which were undoubtedly on our side—though in passing it may be noted that the Soudan and the Cape furnish instances where both availed not against determined savages—it may be well to examine the chief causes which led to this signal success. The result may be described briefly as due to three main causes: To the rapid and successful mobilisation of the Relief Force; to the crushing defeat of the enemy in Swat, on the Panjkora, and in the Jandul Valley; and to the hardy and determined advance of Colonel Kelly's small column from the north. Nor must we forget the stout resistance of the garrison placed perforce in an almost untenable position against overwhelming odds, which thoroughly damped the ardour of the besiegers and paved the way for the effective result obtained by the approach of the relief columns. It was in fact the game of war played on sound principles, and with a fine all-round combination which commanded success.

How nice this calculation had to be will be appreciated by the military student, when he considers how far divergent were the bases from which the two columns had to start, and what immense physical difficulties had to be overcome by each. It does not require much imagination to show that Umra Khan, acting, as he was, on interior lines as against exterior lines, might, if less skilfully assailed, have first thrown his whole force on Colonel Kelly's weak column, entangled in almost impossible defiles; next, with troops elated with victory, have swamped the small garrison of Chitral, already hard pressed and short of food, and then, with a dozen tribes at his back, stirred up to the highest pitch of Mohammedan fanaticism, have turned and assailed the main column under Sir Robert Low. The final result of the campaign must undoubtedly have gone against Umra Khan, but he would have had some signal successes to show in return. It happened to be one of the writer's duties to escort Sher Afzul to India as a prisoner of war, and from conversation held with him it appeared that such in fact had been, in the main, the plan of campaign which Umra Khan had contemplated, and he was frustrated only by the superior combination and strategic skill which directed the march of the relieving columns.

All need for any hurry was now over. Colonel Kelly reached Chitral unopposed on April 20th, and was the first to shake hands with the brave defenders. Sir Robert Low's leading brigade, under General Gatacre, set to work to construct a mule road over the Lowaria Pass, still deep in snow, and a few troops were marched up the Chitral Valley just to show themselves without straining unnecessarily the difficult task of feeding large bodies of troops so far from their base. The campaign ended with one of those gracious messages with which Her Majesty Queen Victoria never failed to acknowledge the gallantry of her Army; whilst in the hearty and soldierly message of the Commander-in-Chief, Sir George White, every man of the Force felt that his services had been appreciated by one who knew well the difficulties that had been overcome, and the stern hardships that had been cheerfully borne.

The British soldier, and his friend and comrade of the Indian army, are accustomed to serve in every degree of climate, and in every nature of country, for an empire of the vast dimensions of the British Empire must needs embrace every variety of climate and country. In the brief and brilliant campaign just concluded perhaps these various conditions were as numerously represented as is possible. There was fierce heat and piercing cold, deluges of rain and blinding storms of snow and hail; the highest mountain system in the world to be climbed, rivers, deep and wide and astonishing in their treacherous strength, to be crossed. With his greatcoat and a blanket for his baggage, the sturdy British soldier and his strapping Indian war comrade, face these many hardships with the cheerful alacrity of men ready and accustomed to overcome unusual difficulties, and to face tremen dous odds by land and sea.

It is seldom, too, that a British campaign does not produce its men of mark and those who have done heroic deeds, nor is this one an exception to the rule, for the names of Sir Robert Low, General Bindon Blood, and General Waterfield stand high in the historic roll of successful generals, whilst Colonel Kelly's brilliant feat of arms has made him famous for ever. But perhaps the deed of all others which appeals most to the soldier's heart was the desperate and successful sortie from Chitral, made by the brave and gallant Harley and his Sikhs on the 17th day of April, 1895.

Sir R. Low and Staff on the Janbatai Pass.

CHAPTER VI

THE DEFENCE OF CHITRAL

Chitral was now relieved; communication with the British officers so long shut up there was once more established, and letters were at last received giving an account of the desperate defence and of all that had occurred since the Chitralis had risen in revolt.

I take up the narrative from the point at which I left it at the close of the first chapter. The Chitralis had then suddenly given up their opposition to Umra Khan and, joining Sher Afzul, who had now allied himself with Umra Khan, had advanced against the British officers established in Chitral fort.

On the 3rd of March, at about 4.30 P.M., news was received by the British officers in Chitral fort that Sher Afzul, with a large force, was approaching. Captain Colin Campbell, of the Central India Horse, and, for the time, Inspecting Officer of the Kashmir Imperial Service Troops, was in command of the troops now in Chitral; and, late in the afternoon though it was, he thought it necessary to go out with a strong reconnoitring force to ascertain the strength and intentions of the Chitrali force. Hostilities between the British and the Chitralis had not yet commenced, and with a large armed force advancing towards the fort it was necessary for the British garrison to take every precaution against being caught unawares. Two hundred Kashmir Infantry under Captains Campbell, Townshend, and Baird, and accompanied by the British Agent, Surgeon-Major Robertson, Lieutenant Gurdon, and Surgeon-Captain Whitchurch, therefore set out from the fort to reconnoitre the Chitrali dispositions. There is no regular town of Chitral, but round the fort, which is merely the residence of the Mehtars, there are scattered over the valley a number of little hamlets, and detached houses, dotted among the cultivated lands which stretch for a distance of about three miles down the valley. These cultivated lands are on some gently sloping ground, from a mile to a mile and a half in width, which runs down from the high, steep hill-sides on the right bank to the river.

Leaving fifty men in the *serai* a quarter of a mile from the fort, and detaching a section under Captain Baird, which Lieutenant Gurdon accompanied, to ascend the hill-sides on the right, Captains Campbell and Townshend advanced for a mile and a half down the valley, towards a house in which it was stated that Sher Afzul had established himself. On arrival at the house it was found that Sher Afzul was not in it, and Captain Townshend then advanced still further down the valley, while Captain Baird's flanking party was strengthened by an additional twenty-five men. Captain Townshend could see a number of men moving about among the trees and houses of a hamlet 500 yards beyond the house which it had been supposed Sher Afzul was occupying; and on the hill-sides which Baird's party were ascending there were some hundreds of the Chitralis. On these hill-slopes firing now commenced, and Captain Townshend concluding that the men he could see in the front moving about in the hamlet were the enemy, opened fire with a section volley. The fire was immediately returned by the enemy, who, being armed with Martini-Henry and Snider rifles, made, says Captain Townshend, most excellent shooting. Among the enemy were several hundred of Umra Khan's men, drilled and trained by pensioners from our own Indian Army; and there were, indeed, many of these pensioners themselves in the force which was now advancing upon Chitral.

Captain Townshend kept his men under cover as much as possible, and, taking advantage, for the purpose, of the boulders and low walls which surrounded the fields, advanced to within 200 yards or so of the hamlet. There was now no more cover in his front, many of his men were hit, and he could see the hamlet towards which he was advancing now crowded with men who were keeping up a well-sustained fire from the walls and loopholes. To advance with the hundred men he had with him, and these not veteran troops of our own army, but untried Kashmir troops armed with worn-out Snider rifles, against superior numbers of a better-armed and more experienced force posted behind walls was an impossibility, and Captain Townshend decided therefore to hold his ground until Captain Baird should move along the hill-slopes to the westward, and so turn the hamlet, and when Baird had done this Townshend would then advance to attack it in front.

But time went on, and Townshend could see no signs of Baird advancing on his flank. On the other hand small parties of the enemy began to overlap him on both flanks and to enfilade him with their fire. His position was now becoming untenable; it was half-past six and would soon be dark, so decisive action of some sort—either an advance or a retirement—had to be carried out at once. At this juncture Captain Campbell arrived and directed that the hamlet should be stormed. The order to reinforce was given but the support of men in rear did not come up, though the order was continually repeated. Captain Campbell then went back to himself bring up the support, while Captain Townshend fixed bayonets preparatory to a charge and kept up a heavy independent fire. The support all this time was lying behind some low walls 150 yards to the rear. Captain Campbell succeeded in bringing on about a dozen men from among them, and then fell shot through the knee just as he was rejoining the advance party. Colonel Jagat Singh, of the Kashmir troops, then went back to try and get more men on, but he could only bring on one or two. So Captain Townshend, finding that to await for further support was useless, went round his men telling them they must rush straight in and take the houses, and he then sounded the charge.

The little party of a hundred men scrambled over the bank behind which they had been lying and advanced to the attack of the strongly-held village to their front. It was a desperate venture, for the enemy were not only in superior numbers and better armed, but they were firing from behind cover, while the troops which the British had now to lead to the attack had to advance across 200 yards of open ground, exposed to fire for the whole distance, and they were men who had never been in action before. Captain Townshend had served in the expedition sent to relieve Khartoum, and had been present in the battles of Gubat and Abu Klea, where Sir Herbert Stewart and Burnaby lost their lives, and he had taken part in the sharp little Hunza campaign in 1891, but he told me that he had never before been under so hot a fire as that which now met his party as they scrambled over the bank. The Kashmir General Baj Singh, a fine old soldier and gentleman, who was always keen to be in the thickest of a fight, and whose keenness had now led him to the front when by rights he should have been more in rear, was shot down on one side of Captain Townshend, while Major Bhikam Singh, another brave old Kashmir officer, was mortally wounded on the other side. Their leaders fallen, the finest troops in the world would have found it hard to face so terrible a fire, and the raw Kashmir infantry could no longer stand before it. Insensibly they shrank under the fire, then crouched down behind stones, till Captain Townshend finding it impossible to carry the charge home in spite of all his endeavours to get the men on abandoned the attempt, and ordered his men back behind the wall from which they had started.

Events had now taken a very serious turn. The British officers were nearly two miles distant from the fort with a handful of disheartened troops in the face of vastly superior numbers of an elated enemy, who were now commencing to overlap them on all sides. The retirement to the fort commenced, and Captain Campbell, even though he was very severely wounded in the knee, mounted a pony and helped to keep the troops in order and steady. This trying manœuvre was effected by alternate parties, the men dribbling off to the rear by word of command while the remainder kept up a heavy fire to keep off the enemy. Captain Townshend always remained with the last party in order to prevent any panic or disorder arising, and in this way the party reached a house about a mile from the fort, where Mr. Robertson was found rallying men who had retired before, and here a short stand was made, while Mr. Robertson, at great risk and exposed to a heavy fire from the enemy now lining the garden walls and houses on every side, rode back to the fort to bring out fifty of Lieutenant Harley's Sikhs to cover the retirement.

It was now quite dark, and the enemy were firing into Captain Townshend's troops from front, flank, and rear, from every hamlet and wall. The Chitralis and Pathans were wild with excitement at the unexpected success of their first encounter with the British, and, carried away in the whirl of enthusiasm, even women hurled down stones upon the retiring troops. Groping their way, and unable at a short distance to distinguish friend from foe, Captain Townshend brought his men along between walls flashing out fire in the darkness till he reached the *serai* near the fort, where he found fifty Sikhs under Lieutenant Harley come out to cover his retreat. Steady as on parade, and calm and unmoved amidst all the excitement around them, Harley and his veterans headed back the storm while the Kashmir troops retired to the fort. Then he and his men slowly retired within the walls also while the enemy closed thickly around, and the investment commenced which was to last forty-seven long days and weary nights.

But when the officers arrived within the walls it was found that two of their number were missing. Neither Dr. Whitchurch nor Captain Baird had yet arrived. It was known that Baird had been desperately wounded, and deep anxiety regarding the fate of him and Whitchurch was felt, when, at about eight o'clock, Whitchurch was seen from the walls staggering along towards the gateway, supporting and half carrying Baird along. At the beginning of the action Baird, with about fifty men, had been sent away on the right to work round the enemy's flank. With his handful of men, and with Lieutenant Gurdon by his side, he ascended the steep rocky mountain slopes which overlook the valley. It is a generally accepted principle of warfare that an attacking party should be divided into an advance party and a support, and this principle was now acted upon; but Captain Baird, with his characteristic zeal, would not remain with the support, and determined on leading the advance himself. And Lieutenant Gurdon, who, being Political Officer was not present in the reconnaissance in a strictly military capacity, was as anxious as Baird to be in front. So the two British officers agreed to go on together with the advance.

But the enemy were now in hundreds on the mountain side firing and hurling down stones upon the little straggling party, who painfully worked their way upward. Captain Baird was mortally wounded in the stomach, many other of his men were also hit, and the party had to be drawn off. Lieutenant Gurdon could not remain long to look after his wounded comrade, for he had to collect the men and conduct their retirement upon the main body.

News was given to Dr. Whitchurch of the misfortune to poor Baird, and a small escort was left to help him home, as no general retirement had yet taken place. All that he could do Dr. Whitchurch did for Baird; but now, as darkness was closing in, it was seen that our troops were retiring, that the enemy were swarming round on all sides, and that even the retreat to the fort was threatened. Whitchurch collected together about a dozen sepoys, and then set off to carry the wounded officer back to the fort. The enemy had penetrated in between him and the main body, and were firing from the houses and garden walls on the way to the fort. The direct road back was therefore quite blocked to him, and Dr. Whitchurch had to take a circuitous route of three miles round. They were exposed to fire for almost the entire way, and had it not been for the darkness nothing could have saved them. On more than one occasion Whitchurch had to lay down his burden, and, at the head of the men he had collected, charge the enemy to drive them from a wall and make a way. Then he would go back, pick Baird up again, and carry him through. Several of the party were killed—how many cannot be correctly ascertained, for in the darkness and confusion it was impossible to ascertain the exact number of his party—and just as they reached the fort, and when in a few minutes more they would have been in safety, Captain Baird was hit for the third time, and wounded in the face. Dr. Whitchurch and the brave Kashmir troops who had remained with him had by their devotion and gallantry brought back their wounded comrade to the other British officers, only to die, indeed, on the following morning, but to die with his brother officers by his side, and where he could be buried by them with the last solemn rites.

Chitral Fort, from the South.

"It is difficult to write temperately about Whitchurch," wrote Mr. Robertson in reporting this action to Government, and men who have themselves gained the Victoria Cross have said that never has it been more gallantly earned than on this occasion by Surgeon-Captain Whitchurch.

The total losses in this day's engagement were twenty-three men killed and thirty-three wounded out of 200, of whom only 150 were actually engaged; and it was with this newly-raised Kashmir regiment depressed by these severe losses, and with their own hearts saddened by the death on the following morning of their brave comrade, that the British officers commenced the defence of the Chitral fort against an enemy correspondingly elated at their success.

The Chitral fort is eighty yards square, with walls twenty-five feet high and about eight feet thick. At each corner there is a tower some twenty feet higher than the wall, and outside the north face on the edge of the river is a fifth tower to guard the water-way. On the east face a garden runs out for a distance of 140 yards, and forty yards of the south-east tower is a summer-house. On the north and west faces were stables and other outhouses.

The fort is built of rude masonry kept together, not by cement or mortar of any description, but by cradle-work of beams of wood placed longitudinally and transversely so as to keep the masonry together. Without this framework of wood the walls would fall to pieces.

It is situated on the right bank of the Chitral River, some forty or fifty yards from the water's edge, and it is commanded from nearly all sides for Martini-Henry or Snider rifle fire, for mountains close by the river rise above the valley bottom. The fort is thus situated for the purpose of maintaining water, and at the time of its construction breech-loading rifles were not in possession of the people of the country, so that the fort could not then be fired into.

The strength of the garrison of the beleaguered fort was 99 men of the 14th Sikhs, 301 men of the Kashmir Infantry, with the following British officers: Surgeon-Major Robertson, British Agent; Captain C. V. F. Townshend, Central India Horse, commanding British Agent's Escort, and Commandant of the fort; Lieutenant Gurdon, Assistant to the British Agent; Lieutenant H. K. Harley, 14th Sikhs; Surgeon-Captain Whitchurch, 24th Punjab Infantry; Captain Campbell, Central India Horse (badly wounded).

There were 11 followers and 27 servants, 16 Punyali levies, 12 native clerks and messengers, 7 commissariat and transport followers, and 52 Chitralis, bringing up the total number within the fort to 543 persons. For these there were supplies which, putting every one in the fort on half rations, would last about two and a half months. There were 300 rounds of ammunition per man for the Martini-Henry rifles of the Sikhs, and 280 rounds per man for the Snider rifles of the Kashmir Infantry.

Photo Van der Weyde, *Regent Street.*

Major C. V. F. Townshend, C.B.

On the 4th of March the enemy commenced offensive action against the British in earnest by firing the whole day long into the fort. On this day, Captain Townshend, who, now that Captain Campbell was wounded and unable to leave his bed, commanded the fort, commenced taking measures for its proper defence. It was a most unfortunate circumstance that affairs had come to a head so quickly, that he was unable to carry out any demolitions of the outhouses, etc., which surrounded the fort. His first care, however, was to do what he could towards carrying out this necessary operation: even though much of the work had to be done under fire, it was necessary to knock down all the garden walls and houses he could, so as to prevent the enemy occupying them and effecting a lodgment, as they thus would be close up to the very walls of the fort. As it was, the besiegers succeeded in occupying the summer-house at the south-east angle of the fort, which was only forty yards distant from the corner tower. The fort is surrounded by numbers of trees of great height, which not only afforded cover to the enemy, but up which it might have been possible for them to climb, and from their higher branches fire into the very interior of the fort, and this formed an additional danger.

Captain Townshend had also to take efficient measures for protecting the way down to the river, for as there was no serviceable well inside the fort it was necessary to obtain every drop of water required by the garrison from the river. This flowed along the north face of the fort and a tower covered the way down to it, but in this wintry season it was low and there was still a space of some thirty yards between the door of this tower and the river's edge. It was necessary, therefore, to construct a covered way from the gate of the tower to the water.

To neutralise the effect of the fire from the hill-sides which, during the whole of the day, came pouring down into the fort, Captain Townshend had to devise some arrangement. Planks, and beams of wood, doors, mule-saddles, boxes, and sacks filled with earth, were piled up as parados to protect the men's backs as they fired from the parapets. There was not, however, sufficient material of a solid description to protect the whole of the interior from the enemy's fire, and where perfect protection could not be made, cover from sight was arranged for, that is to say, cut-up tents, carpets, and curtains were hung across passages and doorways so that the enemy might not be able to see men passing along. If they fired upon these tents and carpets the bullets would of course go through them, but they would be unable to know when anybody was passing along behind them, and it would therefore be scarcely worth their while to keep firing upon these screens on the mere chance of hitting a passer-by. For the parapets, where the besiegers would know that men for certain would be stationed, Captain Townshend arranged sufficient protection of beams of wood, etc.; for the remainder, screens to serve as protection from sight were provided. These first measures occupied the attention of the British officers for the few days following the commencement of the siege.

On the night of the 7th of March the enemy made a determined attack on the water-way. The besiegers were well versed in every art of the attack on such forts as Chitral, for among the numbers were several hundreds of Umra Khan's Jandulis, whose entire lives are occupied in besieging and defending similar forts to that of Chitral. They well knew therefore the importance of cutting off the garrison from its water supply, and this is always the first measure which they attempt. Under cover of darkness they commenced a heavy and well-sustained fire from the trees on the north-west front of the fort, and sent a party of men to effect an entrance to the water-tower. This they actually succeeded in doing, and a small number of them carrying faggots of wood placed these in the interior of the tower, and set fire to them with the object of burning down the entire structure. The garrison, however, were well on the alert, for the men always slept on their alarm posts, and every one was quickly in his place. A well-controlled fire was then commenced on the attacking party. Captain Townshend had given instructions that no independent firing was to be allowed at night, and only section volleys were employed. The enemy's attack was driven off, and water-carriers having been sent out to the water-tower, the fire there was quickly put out.

At the end of the first week of the siege, owing to the admirable arrangements for the protection of the men, there had been only five casualties, but there were now only eighty rifles of the 14th Sikhs and 200 rifles of the Kashmir Infantry fit for duty. These latter, too, were much shaken by their severe losses in the reconnaissance of the 4th of March. They were a new regiment, that action was the first occasion on which they had been under fire, and they had then lost their general and major, and fifty-six killed and wounded out of the total of 250 actually engaged. It was hardly to be wondered at that these men should be depressed at the prospects before them. The siege was likely to be a long one, only half rations could be served to the men, and Captain Townshend saw clearly that under the circumstances he must husband the resources and energy of his men, and watch them and encourage them as much as possible.

The following arrangements besides those already detailed, were now made. First a fort police was established to watch the Chitralis in the fort and prevent them communicating with the besiegers. Amongst these Chitralis were many who were anything but loyal to the British, and who, above everything, desired not to be found on the losing side when the crisis came. They had therefore to be carefully watched to see that they did not attempt communication with their friends outside the fort. Secondly, a system for extinguishing fires was organised. The water-carriers were ordered to sleep with their mussucks (skins) filled with water, and ammunition boxes and any vessels which could be found were also filled with water and placed ready to hand. Patrols were sent round day and night to watch accidents from fire. These precautions were especially necessary on account of the large amount of woodwork inside the fort, and because the walls and towers were built almost as much of wood as of stone. Thirdly, what sanitary arrangements were possible were made. Fourthly, followers, officers' servants, and other non-combatants were organised into parties for carrying water, putting out fire, carrying out demolitions, building up cover from fire, and for every other kind of work for which they could be employed, and so save the regular soldiers. Fifthly, hand mills for grinding were made and men told off for this work. Lastly, Captain Townshend instilled into the minds of all the men that a relieving force would soon come, and then they would be able to sally out and drive back the enemy.

The work of the defence practically devolved upon three officers only—Captain Townshend, Lieutenant Gurdon, and Lieutenant Harley—Surgeon-Major Robertson was engaged in his political duties under flags of truce and so forth in treating and corresponding with the enemy, Captain Campbell was wounded, and Surgeon-Captain Whitchurch was fully occupied with his medical duties. The three officers for the defence therefore took their turn of duty in watches of four hours each, as on board ship. Each, separately, would come on duty for his four hours, rest for eight, and then come on duty again for another four hours, and so on. Theoretically they had eight hours' rest, but in practice it was found that with alarms of attack and with various extra work about the fort to be done, they were more often at rest for four hours and at work for eight, than at work for four and at rest for eight hours, and the work was now all the more trying that they were only on half rations, and that they were never able to sleep undressed. What sleep they got was mostly in the daytime, and even then with all their clothes and generally even their belts on. It was a remarkable fact, however, that in spite of the work they had to go through and the anxieties they must necessarily have had, the sepoys told me when I reached the fort a week after the siege was over, that they never saw on the faces of the officers any sign of their anxiety. Captain Townshend and his officers in fact made a point of, whatever they might feel inwardly, always appearing cheery and in good heart before their men, and upon this depended in no small degree the success of the defence. The Sikhs had sufficient backbone in themselves to keep up heart; they had suffered no loss in the engagement previous to the siege, they were many of them veterans who had fought in many frontier fights, and their native officer had been engaged in the fierce battle at McNeil's Zareba in the Soudan campaign; but the Kashmir troops were young and untried, they were now placed in a position which required all the finest qualities of a soldier, and it was for these especially that it was necessary that the British officers should be able to inspire confidence and hope.

Captain Townshend still continued the work of demolishing the outer walls beyond the main wall of the fort whenever opportunity occurred and he had time to spare. He used the Punyalis for this, and they did it, he says, marvellously quickly. They crept along on their stomachs outside the walls, and with beams of wood pushed down the light outer walls which ran out round the fort. The enemy fired incessantly upon them while the work was being carried out, but nobody was hit. Thirty rounds a day were also fired at the house in which Sher Afzul lived, in order to cause him annoyance, and let him see that the garrison were awake. When an attack was made at night, and there was no firing, the average amount of ammunition expended during the first two or three weeks of the siege was between forty and fifty rounds of Martini-Henry, and twenty or thirty rounds of Snider ammunition daily. To guard against attack by night, arrangements had to be made for lighting up the ground immediately outside the walls of the fort. At first, light balls made up of chips of wood and resinous pine, and soaked in kerosene oil, were lighted and thrown over the walls. But there were not sufficient materials to carry on this method nightly; and the defenders adopted the better plan of building out platforms from the walls, and on these lighting fires which would keep the ground in the vicinity of the fort illuminated for the entire night.

On the night of the 13th-14th of March the enemy made an attack on the east face, outside which is a garden with a number of large trees. They sounded the advance on a bugle, and with much shouting and beating of tom-toms, and keeping up a straggling fire they advanced to the attack. The garrison received them with a brisk fire, and though men had been heard by the defenders shouting to them repeatedly to come and attack the water-way, they gradually slunk off back to their own lines. Finding the enemy still had an intention of attacking the water-way, Captain Townshend further strengthened the way to the river, loopholing and occupying the stables just by the gate.

A letter was received from Sher Afzul on the 15th of March in which the would-be Mehtar said that a party of troops escorting an ammunition convoy had been surrounded and defeated at Reshun; and further, that a British officer, who had come down from Mastuj, had also been taken prisoner, and that he had written a letter to Dr. Robertson, which Sher Afzul would deliver if the British Agent would send some one to receive it. This was the news of the disaster to Captain Ross, and Lieutenants Edwardes' and Fowler's parties. But the officers in Chitral refused to believe it. On the following day, however, a letter written by Lieutenant Edwardes from Reshun on the 13th of March was received, and in it he gave the news of the attack upon his party, and of his being shut up in the post which he had fortified.

On the 19th of March Abdul Majid Khan, Umra Khan's lieutenant, who, with three hundred Jandulis, had been with Sher Afzul during the siege, sent a letter to Dr. Robertson saying that he much regretted that although he had sent off messengers to Reshun to say that peace had been made, a fight had taken place, and that two British officers and nine Mohammedan sepoys had been taken prisoners, and would arrive in Chitral on the following day. On the 20th of March, Lieutenant Edwardes and Fowler reached Chitral, and on the same day a native clerk from the garrison was allowed to come and see them, that he might be able to assure the defenders that there was no mistake about the disasters having occurred.

The news of this unfortunate occurrence much depressed the garrison. They knew that it would not only greatly elate the Chitralis, but would also give into their hands a large quantity of ammunition and engineering stores which might be used against them. Captain Townshend, however, in no way relaxed his efforts in conducting a successful defence, and even during the few days' truce which followed, he worked incessantly at his defences, strengthening the cover to the water-way and constructing a semi-circular loopholed flêche outside the water-door.

Rations were now running short and the officers had to commence eating horse-flesh, killing and salting their ponies. For the next few days and nights the rain poured in torrents, doing much damage to the walls of the fort, a large piece of the parapet on the west front subsiding, and giving the garrison much work in rebuilding it with beams in the evening.

A Union Jack, made up from the red cloth of the sepoys' turbans and other material, was hoisted on the top of the highest tower, the south-west, on the 29th of March, and the garrison considered that from that time onward their luck began to turn. Improved head-cover was made on all the towers, and beams were put up in the stables to protect men going out of the water-gate down to the covered water-way. The top of the water-tower was also strengthened, and its lowest story pierced with loopholes. An attempt was made to send a messenger to Mr. Udny at Asmar, but the enemy was watching so closely, that the man was compelled to return, and not once during the siege were the garrison able to communicate with the outside world.

The amount of ammunition in hand on the 30th of March was 29,224 rounds of Martini-Henry ammunition—*i.e.* 356 rounds per rifle for eighty-two effective sepoys and fourteen Sikhs. Besides this, there were 68,587 rounds of Snider ammunition in hand for 261 effective men of the Kashmir Infantry, that is to say, 262 rounds per rifle for these. There were now fit for duty 343 rifles in all. By these the following guards and pickets had to be furnished:—

Main gate	10	
Parapet	40	(10 on each parapet)
Water pickets	20	
Water tower	25	
Stable picket	20	
Water-gate guard	10	
Guard over Amir-ul-Mulk	6	
Guard over Chitralis at night	4	
Guard on ammunition	6	
Guard on garden gate	6	
Guard on four towers	24	
Total	171	

Thus only 172 rifles were available with which to make a sortie. The strength of the guards had been reduced to the lowest number compatible with safety, and out of 172, at least thirty-five would be required for an inlying picket. The garrison now had supplies to the amount of 45,000 pounds of grain, which would last the number of persons in the fort seventy-four days, or up to the 13th of June, at the rate of 540 pounds a day. Some allowance for wastage would necessarily have to be made. There were only left thirty-six pounds of the clarified butter which native soldiers require so much. And this was kept for the sick and wounded, and for lights at guards in the fort, and even then would only last another twelve days. After that it was known that the already heavy sick-list would be greatly increased, for the men were all the time on half rations, and were getting little else than this clarified butter. Stenches in the stables, too, in which were situated the latrines, were terrible, and a picket of twenty-five men had to be placed there every night, as it lay on the water-way. There was still a little rum left, and some tea, and the Sikhs were given one dram of rum every four days, and the Kashmir Infantry were given a tea ration every third day.

The enemy made a new sangar on the opposite bank of the river on the 31st of March, at a distance of only 175 yards from the place where the garrison had to take the water from the river. The enemy showed the greatest skill in the construction and defence of their sangars, making regular zigzag approaches after the manner of our own engineers, excavating trenches, and building up breastworks of fascines, stones, and earth. The defenders replied by placing screens of tents to conceal the men going down to the water, so that the enemy should not be able to see when any one was on the way to the river's edge. More beams were also put outside the water-gate, to protect the doorway from the fire of the riflemen on the opposite bank of the river.

But the enemy were not only advancing their trenches towards the water-way from the opposite bank of the river, they also now commenced the construction of a covered way to the water from their lower sangar on the north-west front of the fort, close down to the river. This sangar was only about eighty yards from the defenders' covered way to the water. Captain Townshend now commenced further protection for men going to the water, by sinking a trench in the stables. On the 5th and 6th of April, the enemy showed great activity on the south-east corner of the fort, occupying the summer-house only forty yards distant, and they also constructed a large fascine sangar in front of the main gate, at a distance of only forty yards. The garrison commenced loopholing the lower story of this tower to command the east end of the stables, and more loopholes were also made in the stable buildings at the west end. From their proximity, the enemy were able to cause great annoyance to the besiegers, and it was with great difficulty that the defenders were able to keep a proper watch over their proceedings. On the 7th of April, at about 5 A.M., a large number of the enemy opened a heavy matchlock fire from the trees in front of the north tower, and an attack was made on the covered way to the water. The defenders were instantly on the alert, and steady volleys were fired upon the enemy by the Sikhs, which caused them to decamp towards the bazaar.

While this firing was taking place on the western face, the enemy managed with great pluck to place huge faggots and blocks of wood in a pile against the corner of the gun tower on the south-east, and setting alight to it, the tower was soon set on fire, and began blazing up. This was a most serious matter. Captain Townshend immediately sent up the whole of the inlying picket with their greatcoats full of earth, and as much water as could be obtained was brought up to throw down upon the fire. A strong wind was blowing at the time, and though for a moment the fire was got under, it soon blazed up again, the flames mounting up in spaces between the beams and the tower. Dr. Robertson, who was in the tower superintending the putting out of the fire, was wounded at a hole in the wall, and a Sikh shot there the next minute. A sentry of the Kashmir Infantry was also shot. Altogether nine men were wounded, and as the enemy were only forty yards distant, no one could appear above the wall, or at any hole, for the purpose of throwing down earth or water upon the fire raging below, without the risk of being shot. It seemed at one time, therefore, as if it would be impossible to keep down the flames, which were now working right into the tower, and which, if they could not be subdued, would quickly burn down the whole of the woodwork of which so much of the tower is composed, and so cause the whole tower to fall a mass of ruins, and make a great gap in the walls of the fort. Eventually the defenders devised the plan of making a water-spout, which they pushed out through a hole in the corner of the tower, and then pouring in water from the inside, allowed it to pour down on the flames below. In this way, after working for about five hours, the fire was got under, but water was kept pouring down inside the walls all day long, and holes were picked inside the tower to thoroughly clamp it out. To guard against this happening again Captain Townshend made more strict arrangements for watching the ground under the walls, and the better-disciplined Sikhs were put as sentries in place of the men of the Kashmir Infantry.

The Machicoulis galleries were gradually improved and loopholed inside, in a way that all the ground immediately under the tower could be well watched, and a sentry always lay in each of these galleries. Captain Townshend also had heaps of earth collected, and sent up on the parapets, and vessels and ammunition boxes filled with water, placed in every story in each of the towers. The waterproof sheets of the 14th Sikhs were utilised for the purpose of holding water, and all the servants and followers were formed into a fire picket under Surgeon-Captain Whitchurch. Heaps of stones were placed at the top of the towers for the sentries to throw down from time to time in the dark. On the evening of the 8th of April, some red-hot embers and a bundle of faggots were observed quite close to the tower, and it was evident that the enemy had succeeded in rushing up and placing these there while the sentries were being relieved. Captain Townshend accordingly arranged that the sentries should be relieved at a different time from day to day, so that the enemy should be unaware when the relief was taking place. On that day, Captain Townshend demolished some remaining walls left outside the main gate, and he also built a stone loopholed tambour in front of the main gate. This would hold ten men, and from it it was possible to flank the whole of the west front with its two towers.

The Machicoulis gallery in the gun tower was still further improved, and good loopholes were made in the lower story. A hole was dug inside the tower in the floor to the depth of about four feet, and then a shutter-like loophole was made which commanded the ground at the foot of the south face of the tower. Sentries were placed in all of these. Fourteen men were now permanently in this gun tower, and an officer lived in it. The number of men in hospital now were 11 Sikhs, 19 Kashmir Infantry, and 6 others, and there were 49 out-patients besides, making the total number of sick 85.

A great attack upon the water-way was made on the night of the 10th-11th of April. The enemy came rushing in with a tremendous din, yelling, and beating tom-toms, but the defenders immediately sprang to their stations, and fired section-volleys from the parapets. These volleys caused them, as on other attacks, to retreat towards the bazaar, and with a loss of only one man wounded on the part of the defenders, this last assault of the enemy was beaten. On the following day it was noticed that the enemy began playing tom-toms and Pathan pipes, in the summer-house at night, and shouting abuse at intervals. At this time, large parties of the enemy were seen moving away towards Mastuj, and the garrison began speculating upon the approach of a force from Gilgit to their relief. The enemy were indeed moving off to oppose Colonel Kelly, who had now crossed the Shandur Pass and reached Mastuj on his way to Chitral.

On the evening of the 16th of April, it having struck the defenders that the tom-toming, which was so constantly kept up in the summer-house, was intended to drown the sound of the picking of a mine, sentries in the gun tower were warned to be on the alert, and to listen intently. It was thought quite possible that the enemy might have the intention of digging a mine from the summer-house in towards the tower, and right under it, so as to be able to blow it up, and effect an entrance to the fort. At midnight one of the sentries in the lower story of the gun tower, reported that he heard the noise of picking. Captain Townshend himself went up, but could hear nothing. But about 11 A.M. on the morning of the 17th, the native officer in the gun tower reported to him that he could hear the noise of picking quite distinctly. Captain Townshend accordingly again went up, and there could now be no mistake that a mine was being made, and that it had reached to within twelve feet of the walls of the fort. Dr. Robertson came up and listened too; and both officers agreed that the only thing to be done was to rush the summer-house, and destroy the mine, for there was no time to construct a counter-mine, and the enemy's plan must be frustrated at once.

Lieutenant Harley was accordingly told off to command a party of forty Sikhs, and sixty of the Kashmir Infantry, and he was given the following instructions:—"He was not to fire a shot in rushing to the assault, but to use the bayonet only. He was, however, to take forty rounds of ammunition for the purpose of firing upon the enemy after he had captured the summer-house. He was to take with him three powder bags with 110 pounds of powder, and forty feet of powder-hose, and picks and spades. He was to go straight for a gap in the wall of the house with his whole party without any support. Having rushed the place, he was to hold it with part of his men, while with the remainder he was to destroy the mine by pulling down the upright and wooden supports, if any, or by blowing it in if he saw fit. If possible he was to take a prisoner or two."

Captain Townshend summoned the native officers going with Lieutenant Harley, and explained to them the object of the sortie, that they might be able to make it thoroughly clear to their non-commissioned officers and men. All officers carried matches, and one officer was told off to bring up the rear, and see that no man hung back.

At four o'clock in the afternoon of the 17th April, the gate of the east face of the fort was quietly opened, and Lieutenant Harley rushed out at the head of his party. A man was shot on either side of him, even in the short space of eighty yards which they had to cover before reaching the walls of the summer-house. But the enemy had been taken by surprise, and were only able to get off a few hurried shots before Lieutenant Harley and his men were up to the walls, over them, and into their midst. At the time of this unexpected assault there were about thirty Pathans in the house. They bolted down the garden wall, and stopping at the far end, threw out fascines from behind it, and from under this cover, poured a heavy fire into the house. Lieutenant Harley told off a certain number of his men to reply to this, and then sought for the main shaft of the mine. It was found outside the summer-house, behind the garden wall, and thirty-five Chitralis were bayoneted in the mouth of the mine as they came out.

Photo Lafayette, *Dublin.*

Lieutenant H. K. Harley, D.S.O.

While Harley was employed in clearing the mine and holding the summer-house, the enemy, now thoroughly on the alert, began moving in large numbers down to the river-bank and along behind the garden wall towards the water-way, with the intention of making a counter-attack upon it. Captain Townshend having considerable anxiety that an attack made now while a hundred of his men were outside might be successful, lined the parapets and kept an incessant steady fire upon the assailants, while he sent three successive messengers to Lieutenant Harley to hurry up in his work, and warning him that the enemy were gathering round the garden with the intention of either cutting him off, or striking at the water-way. In about an hour's time Lieutenant Harley cleared the mine of the men inside it, and taking down the powder bags placed them in the mine. These were exploded, and the work being completed, Lieutenant Harley rushed back to the fort again, the enemy from the end of the garden keeping up a furious fusillade as they retired. The party lost, altogether, 8 men killed and 13 wounded, *i.e.* 21 killed and wounded out of a total of 100 men. But the work had been accomplished, the mine had been successfully blown up, until it now lay exposed as a trench running up to within ten feet of the fort, and the besiegers had been shown that now, after forty-six days of the siege, the defenders still had pluck and spirits enough left in them to assume a vigorous offensive. It was the most brilliant episode in this gallant defence.

Yet the defenders were not to be carried away by their success, or led into slackening their precautions in any way, and they immediately began to run a subterranean gallery round the tower, to ensure that if the enemy again attempted mining, they must run into it. But now relief was close at hand, and the labours and anxieties of the garrison were soon to cease.

On the night of the 18th of April, a man was heard outside the walls shouting to those inside that he had important news to tell. With great precautions he was let into the fort, and he was then recognised as a man known to the officers. He told them that Sher Afzul and the Janduli chiefs, with all their men, had fled in the night, and that a British force from Gilgit was only two marches distant. The officers at first refused to believe this story, for the news seemed all too good to be true, and they feared that the enemy were merely trying to entrap them into leaving the fort or slackening their watching, and so catching them at a disadvantage. But as no signs of the enemy could be observed, patrols were sent out, and then, as it became apparent that the enemy had really drawn off, the famished British officers, in the first place, showed their satisfaction at their release by sitting down to eat a good square meal. They had so far been only able to eat sparingly even of their horse-flesh, but now, as the siege was over, they could eat as they wished. Then they tried to sleep, but being so excited they found it impossible to do so; so they got up and ate again, calling their first meal "supper," and the second meal "early breakfast." At daylight the next morning, patrols were sent out at some distance from the fort, and the whole place was then found to be deserted, and on the following day Colonel Kelly's little force marched in from Gilgit.

Sketch of South (Gun) Tower, Chitral Fort.

So ended this memorable siege. "The quite exemplary coolness, intrepidity, and energy exhibited by Captain Townshend, and the valour and endurance displayed by all ranks in the defence of the fort at Chitral," said the Commander-in-Chief in India, Sir George White, the defender of Ladysmith, "have added greatly to the prestige of the British arms, and will elicit the admiration of all who read this account of the gallant defence made by a small party of Her Majesty's forces, and combined with the troops of His Highness the Maharajah of Kashmir, against heavy odds when shut up in a fort in the heart of an enemy's country, many miles from succour and support." And the Viceroy, in endorsing the Commander-in-Chief's remarks, said: "That his words will, he feels assured, be deeply felt by every subject of Her Majesty throughout the British Empire. The steady front shown to the enemy, the military skill displayed in the conducting of the defence, the cheerful endurance of all the hardships of the siege, the gallant demeanour of the troops, and the conspicuous example of heroism and intrepidity recorded, will ever be remembered as forming a glorious episode in the history of the Indian Empire and its army." The Viceroy joined with the Commander-in-Chief in deploring the loss of Captain Baird, General Baj Singh, and Major Bhikan Singh, and of so many other brave soldiers who fell in the discharge of their duty. Her Majesty the Queen was pleased to express her gracious approbation of the successful efforts of the troops, and His Excellency the Viceroy in Council tendered to Surgeon-Major Robertson, Captain Townshend, and to the whole garrison, his heartfelt congratulations on their gallant defence of the position entrusted to them, while it was an especial pleasure, His Excellency said, to recognise the devoted aid given by the loyal troops of His Highness the Maharajah of Kashmir.

All ranks in the garrison were granted six months' pay, which reward also fell to the heirs of those killed, in addition to the pensions to which they might be entitled. Surgeon-Major Robertson was created a Knight Commander of the Order of the Star of India; Captain Townshend was made a Companion of the Order of the Bath, and promoted to a Brevet majority; Captain Campbell was given the Decoration of the Distinguished Service Order, and promoted to a Brevet majority; and Lieutenant Gurdon and Lieutenant Harley were both also given the Decoration of the Distinguished Service Order; and, lastly, Surgeon-Captain Whitchurch was awarded that most coveted of all rewards, the Victoria Cross.

CHAPTER VII

COLONEL KELLY'S MARCH

How it came that Colonel Kelly arrived in so timely a way to the relief of the hard-pressed garrison has now to be shown. In the beginning of March alarming reports of the state of affairs in Chitral began to reach Gilgit, the head-quarters of the British Political Agent and of the force of some 3,000 men stationed on this frontier for its supervision and protection. The whole of Lower Chitral was rumoured to be up in arms against the British, and communication with Mr. Robertson and the officers who had two months previously marched from Gilgit to Chitral was now entirely cut off. The flame of rebellion seemed to be spreading, and the gravest anxiety was felt for the safety of the detachments of troops at the various posts on the road and of the several parties which were marching towards Chitral. Mr. Robertson was the British Agent, deputed by the Government of India for the conduct of political affairs on this frontier; but he was now shut up in Chitral, and the control of our relations with the various states round Gilgit and Chitral now, at this critical juncture, devolved upon Captain W. H. Stewart, and it may well be imagined that his task in keeping the various peoples on this frontier quiet and orderly, with the catching influence of the troubles in Chitral, was no easy one.

These excitable and impressionable people of the Hindu Kush spring to arms under little provocation when once the spirit of fighting is abroad. News of what was occurring in Chitral would rapidly reach them, and in every house and hamlet little else would be spoken of. Unless, therefore, the British officers in contact with them could steady them by their influence, there would be a great risk that, thoughtlessly, and rashly, they might rise against us as the Chitralis had done. It hung in a balance whether they would go with us or against us, and it is satisfactory to find that British influence was still so secure even in states like Hunza and Nagar, which had been subdued only three years previously, that when in this crisis Captain Stewart inquired through the political officer in Hunza and Nagar if any more men were willing to enlist temporarily as levies in addition to the ninety men already furnished and now stationed in Ghizr on the way to Chitral, the chiefs of these two states showed the utmost feeling of loyalty, and immediately responded by arriving in Gilgit with some 900 men of all ranks ready to serve Government in any way required. Each man brought a fortnight's supply in order to avoid giving trouble, and the most enthusiastic spirit was displayed by all. A certain number of these men were sent on to Chitral, while others were employed in guarding passes near Gilgit, and as will be seen later on, these men who three short years before were fighting desperately against us, now stood by us in the time of need and rendered to Colonel Kelly in his march to Chitral such service as he repeatedly acknowledged in terms of the highest praise.

Native Levy.

Colonel Kelly was the officer in command of the troops on the Gilgit frontier. He was the colonel of the 32nd Pioneers, a regiment which had a few months previously arrived upon this frontier partly for the purpose of constructing roads and fortified posts, and partly to give a backbone to the force of Kashmir troops who composed the principal part of the garrison. It was the same regiment as afterwards escorted me in Tibet.

The total strength of 3,000 men on this frontier was made up of the regiment of Pioneers of the regular army of India; 200 men of the 14th Sikhs, also of the Indian Army; and three battalions of Kashmir Infantry of 600 men each, and a battery of Kashmir Mountain Artillery. This force in the beginning of March was distributed in the following manner: At Chitral Fort 100 of the 14th Sikhs and 300 Kashmir Infantry; at Mastuj, 100 Sikhs and 150 Kashmir Infantry; at Ghizr, 100 Kashmir Infantry; at Gupis, 140 Kashmir Infantry; at Gilgit, a Kashmir regiment complete. At Hunza and on the line between Hunza and Gilgit, there were 200 Kashmir Infantry, and in Chilas 400. A Pioneer regiment, 800 strong, was located at Bunji, and on the line between there and Chilas.

When it became apparent how critical the state of affairs was, the Government of India saw that it was necessary to move up as many troops as could be spared from Gilgit to afford some relief to the Chitral garrison till the large force under General Low, which was to march from the Peshawur direction, could reach Chitral; but it was not possible to send any large force from Gilgit, for in the neighbourhood of that place there are several small states who had but very recently given trouble, and would now have to be watched, however much loyalty they might show. Hunza had only been subdued at the end of 1891, and Chilas had been brought under submission a year later. There was no sign of disturbance in either of these states, and Hunza especially seemed quiet and contented; but it and the neighbouring state of Nagar had to be guarded, and in Chilas, which is in contact with fanatical and turbulent tribes of the Indus valley, there is always constant risk of insurrection. Under these circumstances, and as it was not known how Yasin and the states to the south of it might act, with Chitral in a state of rebellion close by, it would have been unwise to send away from the Gilgit district any larger force than the 400 Pioneers and two guns which it was now decided Colonel Kelly should take with him to march towards Chitral in order to aid, the garrison to prolong their defence till relief could be sent from the Peshawur direction.

Chitral is 220 miles from Gilgit, and the road between the two places runs through mountainous, difficult country, and crosses a pass 12,400 feet high. The valleys through which the road passes are all very narrow, in just a few places opening out to a width of a mile, but, for the greater part of the distance, only a few hundred yards broad, and in many cases mere defiles with the mountains thousands of feet high on either side and standing out in rocky precipices from the stream at the bottom.

The Shandur Pass is about ninety miles from Chitral and 130 from Gilgit. On the west side of this pass, as has been already mentioned, the whole country was up in arms against the British, and news now reached Gilgit, that besides the garrison of Chitral being shut up, the post of Mastuj was besieged, and, finally, that the detachment of troops under Captain Ross had been annihilated, and that officer killed, and that a second detachment under Lieutenant Edwardes and Fowler had been attacked on the way to Chitral. On the east side of the Shandur Pass is the province of Yasin, formerly independent, but during recent years an integral part of the Chitral state. This province had so far remained quiet, but it could not of course be known whether Colonel Kelly in marching through it would encounter opposition. Even if he did not meet with actual hostility, and if the people were only passively obstructive, his task of reaching Chitral would be an almost hopeless one, for both in the matter of supplies and of transport he must of necessity largely depend upon the people of the country through which he passed.

On March 23rd and 24th Colonel Kelly's force set out from Gilgit, the news having just previously reached them of the annihilation of Captain Ross's party. The first detachment which Colonel Kelly himself accompanied was composed of 200 men of the 32nd Pioneers under Captain Borrodaile, with Lieutenants Bethune (afterwards killed in Tibet) and Cobbe, and Surgeon-Captain Browning-Smith; and the second detachment of 200 Pioneers under Lieutenants Petersen and Cooke. Two guns of the Kashmir Mountain Battery also accompanied the latter detachment.

It was with this little force that Colonel Kelly started on his venturesome journey to succour the Chitral garrison, to restore British prestige, to steady the frontier, to keep those who were wavering from flooding over to the opposite side, and to give heart to those who still trusted and looked to the British. And it may be well here to explain, for the benefit of those not acquainted with our Indian Army, who the men were whom Colonel Kelly was now taking with him on this march. The Pioneer regiment, of which he was taking a wing, is composed of Sikhs from the Punjab. The regiment is organised and equipped for the special purpose of making roads and doing light pioneer work in advance of the army. It is drilled, and on service fights as an ordinary infantry battalion, but it can be used as well for the important work of road-making and construction of out-posts as for ordinary fighting purposes. The men were then armed with Martini-Henry rifles, and carried in addition, each man, a pickaxe, a shovel, or some other tool required for pioneer purposes. Colonel Kelly's force, to save transport, which was very difficult to obtain, travelled without tents. Each sepoy was allowed fifteen pounds of baggage, and he carried a greatcoat and eighty rounds of ammunition, and wore a short "poshtin" (sheepskin coat). The guns of the Kashmir Mountain Battery were 7-pounders of a rather antiquated pattern. The officers and men of the battery belonged to the army of the Maharajah of Kashmir, and for the last few years had been drilled under the supervision of British officers.

At Gupis (sixty-five miles from Gilgit), where there is a small masonry fort, built in the previous year by Kashmir troops under the supervision of Captain Townshend as an advanced post in the direction of Chitral, Lieutenant Stewart, Royal Artillery, joined Colonel Kelly, to be with the two guns brought from Gilgit.

Sepoy, 32nd Pioneers.

Five marches further on at Ghizr a small detachment of sixty Kashmir Infantry under Lieutenant Gough, forty Kashmir Sappers and Miners under the supervision of Lieutenant Oldham, R.E., and 100 levies from Hunza-Nagar, were stationed.

Ghizr is 10,000 feet above the sea-level, and is a small village occupied by a hardy and somewhat independent set of people. Here it was that Colonel Kelly's chief difficulties were likely to commence. He had been able to get so far without encountering any serious obstacle. The people of Yasin had shown no hostility, and Ghizr had been reached without mishap; but here at Ghizr snow lay deep on the ground, and at the time of Colonel Kelly's arrival had been falling steadily for five days previously. The Shandur Pass (two marches ahead) had to be crossed, and the British officers had to bear in mind that if the pass could not be crossed, or if any sort of disaster befell them on the opposite side, there was the almost certainty that the loyalty of the people of Yasin in their rear would not stand the test of further trial, and that the Yasinis, believing that the Chitralis in rebellion on the western side of the pass must be in the ascendant, would begin to trim their sails to join them so as to save their own necks.

On the 31st of March both detachments of Colonel Kelly's force had reached Ghizr, and in spite of the heavy snowfall and of the unpromising look of matters, it was decided to push on the next day towards Chitral, for the British officers in the fort there had now been shut up for four weeks, and it was urgently necessary to press forward as rapidly as possible to their aid.

On April 1st, Colonel Kelly left Ghizr with the whole force, but difficulties commenced at once. The start, which was to have been made at 7 A.M., did not take place for three hours later on account of the coolies required for the carriage of the supplies in crossing the pass having absconded. For some hours the force plodded resolutely through the snow, but at about 2 P.M. it became apparent that, eager as they were to push on to the relief of their comrades in Chitral, it would be impossible to proceed with the means at their disposal. What was most necessary was to take on the guns; for the mere rumour that Colonel Kelly was bringing guns with him had been sufficient to produce the strongest moral effect upon the Chitralis, unaccustomed as they were to these weapons. The Chitralis might formerly have dreaded the regular troops of the Indian Army, but they had already annihilated two detachments of these troops, and were now engaged in besieging others, and Colonel Kelly's Pioneers alone might not have been able to produce that strong moral effect which was so necessary; but if guns could be brought over, the Chitralis would certainly be terrified, and Colonel Kelly was above everything anxious that the two guns he had brought from Gilgit should accompany him over the pass.

Here, however, just at the critical time, there seemed no possibility of his being able to carry out his object. The gun-carriages and the ammunition boxes, etc., are carried on mules, and, on this march from Ghizr towards the pass, it was found that the mules could scarcely move through the snow; they were floundering about in it, up to their bellies, and in the afternoon it became apparent that it was no longer possible to take them any further, much less to bring them over the pass. This was the state of affairs on April 1st, as Colonel Kelly was marching out from the last village towards the pass. Colonel Kelly had now, therefore, to decide whether the enterprise should be abandoned for the present and a more favourable season awaited, or whether a part of his force should be sent to cross the pass while the remainder returned to quarters at Ghizr. He elected the latter arrangement, and while the guns and 200 of the Pioneers, with 50 Nagar levies, returned with him to Ghizr, 200 of the Pioneers, with Captain Borrodaile, Lieutenant Cobbe, and Surgeon-Captain Browning-Smith, and 40 Kashmir Sappers and Miners under Lieutenant Oldham, R.E., with 50 Hunza levies, remained at Teeru, a small hamlet about seven miles beyond Ghizr in the direction of the pass.

On the 2nd of April snow fell the whole day, and Captain Borrodaile, with the detachment which was to make the first attempt to cross the pass, had to remain patiently at Teeru. In the afternoon Lieutenant Stewart, R.A., arrived from Ghizr again with the two guns. It was impossible to carry these guns over on mules, but the Pioneers, unwilling to leave them behind, had themselves volunteered to carry them over on their backs. They had gone to their officers and said, that in addition to their own rifles and ammunition, pioneer equipment, and kit, they would guarantee that they would themselves transport the guns with the gun-carriages, ammunition, etc., over the pass. A detachment of the 4th Kashmir Rifles, under Lieutenant Gough, had also volunteered to assist in this work, and they, too, now arrived in Teeru.

This splendid offer, which showed so clearly the noble spirit which animated the troops, was eagerly accepted by the British officer, and on the 3rd of April Captain Borrodaile set out from Teeru to cross the pass with his spirited little body of native troops. The snow was very deep and the work of marching through it excessively heavy. A more arduous task than the men had voluntarily set themselves to do, it would be hard to imagine; but hard though it was, to their everlasting credit, the feat was successfully accomplished. Sledges were at first tried, but they had to be given up as useless. Narrow as these sledges were, a single man track was still narrower and extremely uneven with great holes every few steps, so that they could not be hauled easily and were abandoned. All day long the men struggled through the snow with the guns, till between nine and ten o'clock in the evening it was so dark that the track could scarcely be seen, and it was then decided that if the men were to get in at all, those behind would have to drop their loads. This was accordingly done, ammunition boxes, etc., were stacked in the snow, and the troops marched on to Langar, the camping spot at the foot of the pass.

There was only one small hut in which the more exhausted men were placed, and the remainder being without tents had to remain in the open for the whole night. The men with Captain Borrodaile were Sikhs from the plains of the Punjab, brought up for generations in one of the hottest climates in the world, and they were now called upon, after the severe struggles of this and previous days, to spend a night on the snow at nearly 12,000 feet above sea-level, and with the thermometer somewhere about zero (Fahrenheit). Sleep for most of them was out of the question; the men as far as possible gathered round small fires which had been made up from the brushwood to be obtained near the camping spot, and wearily awaited the dawn and final struggle of the coming day.

On the following morning Captain Borrodaile set off for the pass; but as it had now become clear to him that if his men were to attempt to carry over the guns as well as their own kit, they would inevitably break down altogether, he decided to leave Lieutenants Stewart and Gough behind, and directed these two officers to employ that day in bringing the remaining loads into camp and storing them there till either Captain Borrodaile could send back assistance from the opposite side of the pass, or until aid could come from Ghizr. Captain Borrodaile's men found the task of crossing the pass just heart-breaking; every few steps they would sink in through the snow, although some sort of a track had been beaten out by the levies going on in front. At times they would fall in almost up to their armpits, so that they had to be pulled out by their comrades. This was fearfully trying to men loaded as they were, to men too who had passed an almost sleepless night and started for this, the crisis of the enterprise, thoroughly exhausted.

By the time the party had reached the middle of the pass men were falling out in twos and threes, sitting down in the snow as if they were on the point of giving up the struggle. The heavy loads which they had to carry, rifles, ammunition, haversacks, greatcoats, etc., were weighing them down and utterly exhausting them. The snow was from three to five feet deep and quite eighteen inches of it was soft and fresh. At the same time the sun was pouring down upon the men, and adding to their discomfort by the glare which it produced from the white surface of the snow. Although all the men were provided with blue spectacles, many cases of snow-blindness occurred. The absence of water too caused the men additional suffering. Little relief was afforded them from sucking snow, and many were afraid to do that, thinking it might produce some bad influence. So exhausted were the men that it seemed at one time to the British officers that it would be necessary to spend another night on the snow, but at about 5.30 the advance guard came to the end of the flat part of the top of the pass, and the descent was at last commenced. News was at once passed along the line and fresh spirit came into the men. They pulled themselves together for a final effort, and when a little further on some water was obtained, they began to step out briskly. A critical time had now been reached; the party were descending the western side of the pass into the part of the country which had for a month now been up in open arms against the British. It was known that there was a village at the foot of the pass, and it was quite possible that Captain Borrodaile's exhausted troops might find resistance offered them here at the very culminating point of their troubles. Captain Borrodaile had therefore to send on his few levies to scout and discover if the enemy were in any force in the village of Laspur, at the foot of the pass, and to report on the state of affairs there. Fortunately no opposition was met with, for the Chitralis had scarcely expected that the troops would be able to cross the pass in its then condition, and at about 7.30, nearly twelve hours after the first start had been made from Langar, Laspur was reached.

In this straggling village a few inhabitants were found, who immediately came in to pay their respects, as, 200 men in their midst, even though they were so exhausted, were to be propitiated. Captain Borrodaile's party then made themselves snug for the night in the various buildings and outhouses, improvised a few rough defences against a night attack, and then prayed that for this night at least, after all their terrible exertions, they might be left in peace.

On the next morning (April 5th) Captain Borrodaile, having seized a number of inhabitants of the village, sent them back over the pass to Langar to help Lieutenant Stewart and Lieutenant Gough to carry over the guns and the remaining loads, which had been left on the near side of the pass. These two officers, with the small detachment of Kashmir Infantry, succeeded in their task, and to them is due the credit of performing this splendid feat of carrying guns over a high pass in, perhaps, its worst condition, and bringing them down into Chitral territory to give so important a help to Colonel Kelly's force. On the 4th, Surgeon-Captain Browning-Smith made an examination of the men who had crossed the pass, and found twenty-five cases of frost-bite and thirty of snow-blindness. These were fortunately not severe, but it was evident that even one more day's work such as these troops had had to undergo would have quite incapacitated the force.

We must now try and realise what was the position of this small detachment which Captain Borrodaile had with such resolution brought over the Shandur Pass. They were now in the presence of an enemy elated with success, and behind them this terrible pass, practically cutting off their retreat. The village of Laspur had to a certain extent been surprised, though two spies stationed on the pass had been observed by Captain Borrodaile's party, but a considerable number of Chitralis were known to be in the valley lower down, and an attack on Captain Borrodaile might be made at any moment. Colonel Kelly's instructions to Captain Borrodaile were to entrench himself on arrival, return his coolies, and endeavour to open up communication with the garrison of Mastuj, two marches below Laspur, who were besieged by the Chitralis.

On the evening of April 5th a short reconnaissance was made below the camp, as the levies had brought back information that a small body of the enemy had been seen.

On April 6th a reconnaissance in force was made by Captain Borrodaile to Gasht, twelve miles distant; the two guns and one hundred and twenty of the pioneers taking part in the movement. Gasht was reached without opposition, and the villages on the route were found almost deserted, but Captain Borrodaile's troops were able to seize some thirty inhabitants and twelve ponies to serve for transport purposes. Captain Borrodaile returned to Laspur the same night, and he then found Colonel Kelly with Lieutenant Beynon, his staff-officer, and about fifty levies had crossed the pass and arrived in Laspur.

On the 7th the troops rested and prepared for an advance on the following day.

On the 8th the force reached Gasht unopposed, and a small reconnaissance in the evening showed that the enemy were occupying a strong position across the valley at a place called Chokalwat, a few miles below. This position Colonel Kelly decided to attack the next morning. The Chokalwat position is one of great natural strength, and of that order which is generally described as impregnable. Any one looking at it would say that here a hundred men could keep a whole army at bay. On each side of the valley mountains tower up thousands of feet in rugged precipices; a river flows along it, and the only road leads either along the bottom of a stone-shoot, down which the enemy from above could hurl rocks on any force passing beneath; or else over the river and by a zigzag path up some cliffs, the edges of which the enemy had lined with sangars or stone breastworks. At accessible points on the mountain sides the enemy had also constructed these breastworks, and if the Chitralis were determined to offer Colonel Kelly at all a resolute opposition, he might have been brought to a standstill here at his first contact with the enemy, and his main object of affording speedy relief to the garrison in Chitral would be frustrated. In the Hunza campaign of 1891, our troops had been kept at bay for nearly a fortnight in just such another position. The Hunza men were few of them armed with rifles, while the Chitralis had numbers of breech-loaders, and it was not difficult to imagine that a check might here be offered to the relief force, and a check, anything else indeed but complete success, would have involved the British in most serious trouble, and might have caused the people all along the lengthy line of communications to show hostility.

On the morning of April 9th, at 10.30 A.M., Colonel Kelly advanced to the attack of this position. In the early morning Lieutenant Beynon with the Hunza levies were sent up the high hills on the left bank of the river, so as to turn the right of the enemy's position and attack in rear. The Punyalis were ordered up the hills on the right bank to turn out the men above the stone-shoots on that side. The enemy's position consisted of a line of sangars blocking the roads from the river up to the alluvial fan on which they were placed. The right of the enemy's position was protected by a snow glacier which descended into the river bed, and also by sangars which were built as far up as the snow-line on the hill-side. The road down the valley led on to the alluvial fan, the ascent to which was short and steep—it was covered with boulders, and intersected with *nullahs*. The road led across this fan and then along the foot of the steep, shaly slopes and shoots within 500 yards of the line of sangars crowning the opposite side of the river bank, and totally devoid of any sort or description of cover for some two miles. It could also be swept by avalanches of stones set in motion by a few men placed on the heights for that purpose.

The force with which Colonel Kelly advanced to the attack of this position consisted of 190 men of the 32nd Pioneers, two guns of the Kashmir Mountain Battery, 40 Kashmir Sappers and Miners, and 50 levies—in all, 280 men. Colonel Kelly considered that any delay to wait for the second detachment of his troops, who were on their way over the Shandur Pass, would only give the enemy an opportunity for collecting in greater strength, and for improving the fortification of their position, and he decided therefore to attack at once, and advanced in the following order:—A half company of 32nd Pioneers formed the advance guard, and these were followed by the forty Kashmir Sappers and Miners, a half company of the 32nd Pioneers, the two guns which were carried by coolies, and the other company of the 32nd Pioneers completed the main body. The baggage, under escort of the rear guard, remained at Gasht till ordered forward to the action.

The advance was made up to the river where the bridge had been broken by the enemy, but was now sufficiently repaired by the Sappers and Miners for the passage of the infantry. The guns forded the river, and the force ascended to the fan facing the right sangar of the enemy's position. Colonel Kelly's plan was for the advance guard to leave the road and form up on the highest part of the fan facing A sangar, which was to be silenced by volley firing and the guns. He also proposed to adopt the same course with regard to B sangar, when an opportunity should offer for the infantry to descend into the river bed and ascend the left bank to enfilade the enemy in the remaining sangars, which it was expected would be vacated as soon as Lieutenant Beynon's flank attack with the levies had developed.

The advance guard of the Pioneers formed up at about 800 yards from the position, while the main body followed in rear. The Pioneers then advanced to the attack—one section of C company extended, another section of the same company in support; two sections of C company and the whole of A company in reserve. The guns then took up a position on the right and opened on A sangar at a range of 825 yards. As the action progressed the supporting section of C company advanced and reinforced the remaining half of C company, which also advanced, and leaving sufficient space for the guns, took up their position in the firing line on the extreme right. Volley firing was first opened at 800 yards, but the firing line advanced 150 to 200 yards as the action progressed. At a later stage one section of A company was pushed up to fill a gap on the right of the guns in action in the centre of the line. A few well-directed volleys and accurately-aimed shells soon caused the enemy to vacate A sangar in twos and threes, till it was finally emptied. Meanwhile Lieutenant Beynon with his levies had found his way up the hill-sides on the left bank of the river, and as the Pioneers advanced across the fan Lieutenant Beynon drove the enemy from their sangars on the hill-sides. As soon as the enemy had been cleared from A sangar, Colonel Kelly directed his attention to B sangar, and attacked it in a similar manner, and just as the enemy had fled from the first, they now vacated B sangar also. At the same time those of the enemy who had been driven from the positions on the hill-side came streaming down into the plain, and a general flight ensued. An advance of Colonel Kelly's whole force was then made down the precipitous banks to the bed of the river. This advance was covered by the fire of the reserves; the river was forded, and sangars A and B occupied. The guns were then carried across, and the whole line of sangars having been vacated, the column was re-formed in the fan, and the advance was continued to a village one and a half miles further along the bed of the river, and there a halt was made.

So terminated the first successful action with the enemy. It was carried out, says Colonel Kelly, with the extreme steadiness of an ordinary morning parade; the volleys being well directed and properly controlled. The action lasted but one hour, and the casualties on the side of the British were only one man of the 32nd Pioneers severely wounded, and three Kashmir Sappers slightly wounded. The strength of the enemy was computed at from 400 to 500 men, and they were armed with Martini-Henry and Snider rifles. Several dead were found in the sangars, and the loss of the enemy was estimated to have been from fifty to sixty men.

After a short halt the troops continued the advance by the left bank of the river till within three miles of Mastuj, where the river was forded. Here, drawn up on the crest of an alluvial fan above the river, were seen the British garrison of Mastuj, who had been shut up in the fort for eighteen days, but who had, on hearing the firing of Colonel Kelly's troops, and seeing the enemy gradually vacating their position round the fort, now come out to join hands with the relieving force.

At 5 P.M. Colonel Kelly's force reached Mastuj itself, and so in a single day a successful action had been fought, the beleaguered garrison of Mastuj relieved, and another march made in the direction of Chitral.

Lieutenant Moberly, who was in command at Mastuj, was now able to relate the story of his adventures since his investment by the Chitralis. In a previous chapter the story of the disasters to the parties under Captain Ross and Lieutenant Edwardes has been told. These detachments had in the beginning of March set out from Mastuj for Chitral, but no news of what had happened to them, or of what was occurring in Chitral reached Lieutenant Moberly. He had sent messengers down to Buni three times, but each time they were cut off. On March 10th Captain Bretherton (who was afterwards drowned in the Brahmaputra on the way to Lhasa), the Deputy-Assistant Commissary-General for the Gilgit force, arrived in Mastuj with a detachment of 100 Kashmir Sepoys from Ghizr, and so brought up the Mastuj garrison to a total strength of 170 men. Sixty more men arrived from Ghizr on the 13th, and on the 16th Lieutenant Moberly, who had been trying for some days to obtain coolies to enable him to march down to Buni to ascertain the fate of Captain Ross's party, set out from Mastuj with 150 Kashmir Infantry. No coolies had been obtained, and each man had to carry his poshtin (sheepskin coat), two blankets, 120 rounds of ammunition, and three days' cooked rations. Sanoghar, a village eight miles below Mastuj, was reached that day, but no longer march could be made, as a bridge over the river had to be repaired. Fifty Punyali levies had joined Lieutenant Moberly, and on the next morning he left for Buni. This he reached at 5 P.M., and found there Lieutenant Jones and the seventeen survivors of Captain Ross's party, and thirty-three men who had been left in Buni by Captain Ross before his march to Koragh. Lieutenant Jones had been unable to proceed towards Mastuj for fear of attack on the difficult road there, and had remained on in Buni trying to communicate with Lieutenant Moberly, and hoping that relief might be sent him.

This relief Lieutenant Moberly at no small risk, for there are many points on the eighteen miles of road between Mastuj and Buni where his retreat might have been cut off, had now gallantly brought. But Buni was no place in which to stay longer than was absolutely necessary. It is an open village; there is no defensible post in it, and above everything there were not supplies sufficient to last any length of time. The enemy were already in strength at Drasan, a few miles distant on the opposite bank of the river, and Lieutenant Moberly heard that they intended to cut off his retreat that very night at the Nisa Gol, a strong position on the way between Buni and Mastuj. Lieutenant Moberly heard also that the enemy were collecting on the road between Mastuj and Gilgit, and that no more of our own troops had yet started from Gilgit.

He had no choice left but to return to Mastuj immediately. So after remaining there only two hours he set out at 7 P.M. on the 17th on his return journey. A party had been previously despatched to seize the bridge over the river and the difficult piece of cliff along which the road passes, and the Punyali levies had been sent forward to if possible prevent the enemy from occupying the Nisa Gol position. These precautionary measures were successfully carried out; the enemy did nothing more than follow the party along the path, and Lieutenant Moberly after marching steadily all night halted for a few hours at dawn, and proceeded on to Mastuj, which he reached in safety about 10 A.M. on the 18th, having thus by a bold and carefully-planned march rescued Lieutenant Jones's party from probably the same fate that befell Lieutenant Edwardes's party. He did this, too, just in the nick of time, for only a few hours after he had left Buni, the enemy arrived there in force, and afterwards occupied the Nisa Gol position.

On the three days following his return to Mastuj, Lieutenant Moberly and Captain Bretherton were busily occupied in cutting down trees, from them making up fence-work round the fort, and completing defensive arrangements generally. The Hunza-Nagar levies, to the number of one hundred, were sent back to Ghizr on the other side of the Shandur to reinforce that post and be in communication with Gilgit. On the 25th news reached Mastuj that Lieutenants Fowler and Edwardes had been captured by the Chitralis. The enemy were now closing round the fort. A reconnaissance which Lieutenant Moberly had taken out on the 22nd showed that about six hundred of them were building and holding sangars at Chokalwat position, a few miles above Mastuj on the way to Gilgit, and a regular blockade of the fort now commenced.

Mastuj fort is about ninety yards square, and is built of masonry and woodwork, in the same manner as are all the forts in these parts. The walls are about twenty-five feet high, but at the time of the siege were in a dilapidated condition, for the place had only been temporarily occupied by the British as a residence for the political agent and his escort pending the decision of the Government as regards our permanent policy towards Chitral. And unfortunately a very severe earthquake in the previous year had shaken the walls very nearly to pieces. At that time I was the political agent there, and a little incident which occurred while the earthquake was taking place is worth recording as an instance of the steadiness of the native troops. Lieutenant Gurdon, the officer in command of the escort of Sikhs, and myself were seated in a room of the fort when we suddenly felt the whole place shaking. But earthquakes are common in Chitral and we did not at first move, till we heard stones crashing down outside and the whole room tossing about like a cabin on board ship. Then we dashed out of the door to the courtyard, and as we did so passed a sentry, who quietly proceeded to present arms in salute as if nothing was happening. The mountains round were in a cloud of dust from the avalanches of rock set rolling down their sides by the earthquake, and the rickety walls of the fort tumbling on all sides; but all this did not disturb the Sikh sentry; his sense of discipline was so ingrained that he saluted as usual, in the ordinary, everyday manner.

The Mastuj fort is situated on the edge of a sloping plain running down from the hill-side which at one point approaches to within about 400 yards of the fort. The enemy occupied a row of houses some 300 yards from the fort, which they loopholed, and from these commenced firing upon the fort. They also built sangars at a distance of 800 yards, but the garrison succeeded in silencing their fire by aiming volleys into them; and on one occasion Punyali levies were sent out at night to whitewash the loopholes of sangars out of which the enemy had been driven during the day, so that it would be possible for the garrison to aim correctly if the enemy attempted to reoccupy them. The enemy did subsequently come back to the sangars, but only to be driven out again by the carefully-aimed fire from the garrison.

On another occasion the Chitralis had built a sangar on the hill-side and from it wounded two ponies in the inside of the fort. The enemy were armed with Martini-Henry and Snider rifles and could fire from long ranges into the fort. It was necessary therefore to dislodge them from the sangar, and the Punyali levies were sent early one morning to destroy it before it had been occupied for the day by the enemy. Some days afterwards a sangar was built about 300 yards below the fort, but Lieutenant Moberly moved out with a party of eighty sepoys and rushed it. The enemy only fired a few shots, and then retired into some houses from which they harassed the return of the party. The sangar, which was found to be strongly built of fascines and stones, was destroyed.

All this time the Chitralis had been trying to induce Lieutenant Moberly to come out under the promise of a safe conduct to Gilgit, and he was assured that Sher Afzul, the pretender to the throne of Chitral, had no wish to fight the British. Had Lieutenant Moberly listened to these insinuating advances he would undoubtedly have been captured as soon as he came outside, and he acted wisely to wait for the relief which, though he was not aware of it, was now near at hand. On the 9th of April large numbers of the enemy were observed to be moving off, and Lieutenant Moberly took out his men to follow them up and harass them. Then it was that he met Colonel Kelly's force marching in to the relief of the garrison. The siege was now at an end; the tables were turned, and relieving and relieved forces now marched down to succour Chitral.

From the 10th to the 12th of April Colonel Kelly halted in Mastuj to allow of arrangements for supplies and transport for the further march to Chitral to be made, and to await the arrival of a second detachment of the troops catching up from the Shandur Pass. On the 11th of April this detachment arrived accompanied by Surgeon-Captain Luard with the Field Hospital, which was now established at Mastuj; and on the same day a reconnaissance was made by the levies in the direction of Chitral, as the enemy were reported to be holding a strong position a few miles below Mastuj. On the 12th of April a further reconnaissance was made by Lieutenant Beynon, the staff-officer, and an accurate sketch of the enemy's position brought back by him, which enabled Colonel Kelly to settle the course of his action. The position was generally considered to be impregnable, and the late Mehtar of Chitral had, standing on the very spot, himself explained to me its natural strength, and affirmed that it was one of the strongest positions in his country. In Chitral all the positions in the mountain valleys are well known and are regularly occupied in each successive invasion which occurs, and this position, Nisa Gol, is the one which has been selected from time immemorial by the Chitralis in the defence of their valley.

The valley of the Chitral River at the Nisa Gol position is about a mile wide, and is bounded on either hand by steep rocky mountains, rising for several thousand feet above the river. On the left bank especially the mountain sides are very precipitous, and up against these the Chitral River runs. On first looking down the valley it appears as if, in between the mountains, there was nothing but a smooth plain running down from the right-hand side, and it is not till one is actually on it that it is discovered that the seemingly open plain is cleft by a *nullah* between 200 and 300 feet deep, and with absolutely perpendicular sides. The *nullah* is the Nisa Gol, and only one path leads across it, that of the road to Chitral, and this path the enemy had now cut away. There had been a small goat-track across this *nullah* at another point, but the enemy had now entirely obliterated it. Sangars had also been erected at the head of these paths and along the right bank of the *nullah*. These sangars were sunk into the ground and head-cover was provided by a covering of timber and stones. On the left of their position they had sangars on the spur of the hill in a general line with the sangars on the plain, and on the hill parties of men were stationed to throw down stones. On the right of their position across the Chitral River, and slightly in advance of the general line, they had another line of sangars on a spur stretching away high up into the snow-line.

Such was the position which Colonel Kelly had now to attack, and in it the Chitralis had collected to the number of about 1,500 men under their chief leader, Mohamed Isa, to make their principal stand, so as to prevent Colonel Kelly joining hands with the British garrison in Chitral.

Colonel Kelly, reinforced by the garrison of Mastuj, now had with him 382 Pioneers under Captain Borrodaile, two guns under Lieutenant Stewart, 100 Kashmir Infantry under Lieutenant Moberly, 34 Kashmir Sappers and Miners under Lieutenant Oldham, R.E., and 100 Hunza and Punyali levies. With this force he advanced from Mastuj at 7 A.M. on the 13th of April. His plan was to send on an advance guard, which, on gaining the plain which the enemy's position bisected, would make its way well up to the right where the ground favoured an advance under cover to within 500 yards of the ravine, whose further bank was occupied by the enemy. This advance guard was ordered to direct its attack on the sangar on the right with well-directed volleys till the guns and the remainder of the force could come into position. As soon as the advance guard could silence the fire in this sangar, which commanded the advance across the plain, the main sangars along the banks of the ravine were to be fired upon. At the same time levies were to make their way high up in the ravine nearer its source in the mountains on Colonel Kelly's right, to find some path by which the enemy's left could be turned.

The advance guard, composed of A company, at about 10.30 A.M. deployed into line and advanced in extended order when within 900 yards of the position, the C company following soon after prolonging the line to the right. Each of these two formed their own supports, E and G companies were in reserve, marching in column of half companies forming single rank, and opening out into one pace as they advanced. Reinforcements being called for, E company advanced and prolonged the line to the right, G company being called up similarly later on, formed the extreme right of the firing line. The levies were well on the right, high up towards the head of the ravine. While these movements were being executed, the guns came into action at a range of 500 yards, firing common shell, and knocking down the wall of the sangar to a height of about three feet, and so, for a short time, silencing the fire from it. The guns were afterwards advanced to a distance of 275 yards from the enemy's main sangar.

The infantry having deployed, A and C companies kept the enemy engaged directly in front along the main line of sangars, the latter company occasionally directing its fire half right against the sangars on the hills in that flank. The fire of E and G companies was almost entirely directed against the hill sangars—occasional volleys being directed on small parties of the enemy occupying hill tops from 800 to 900 yards distance. The general average distance at which firing was opened to the front was from 250 to 300 yards. As soon as the guns had silenced the fire from the sangars on the hill-sides to the right, they shelled at ranges from 875 yards to 1,200 yards the sangars along the edge of the ravine.

The existence of the goat-path across the ravine already referred to was now reported to Colonel Kelly by his staff-officer Lieutenant Beynon, and Colonel Kelly accordingly directed that an attempt should be made to make it practicable so that the force might cross by it. Some ladders had been brought with the force for the special purpose of crossing the ravine, and the Kashmir Sappers under Lieutenant Moberly were sent forward with Lieutenant Beynon to carry out the work. The scaling-ladders were lowered down the sides of the ravine by means of ropes, and after half an hour's work a track was made by which the bottom of the *nullah* could be reached and an ascent by the goat-track on the further side assured. The troops then descended into the *nullah,* and eventually a party of about fifteen succeeded in climbing the opposite bank, which they reached almost simultaneously with the levies, who had now worked their way round by the right, turned the enemy's left and reached the sangars on the hill-side. The appearance of these bodies on the enemy's left caused a general flight, and they streamed out of their sangars in a long line, with the guns firing at ranges from 950 to 1,400 yards, and under volleys of rifle fire from the infantry, Colonel Kelly then ordered a general advance across the *nullah* by the road leading to Chitral. A company, as soon as it could be mustered, was sent in pursuit, but the enemy's flight was extremely rapid, and they succeeded in effecting a retreat towards Drasan and over the hill-sides on the right bank of the river.

Colonel Kelly in reporting this action said that he could not speak too highly of the extreme steadiness and bravery of the troops during the course of the action, which lasted two hours, and during which they were subjected to a very heavy and trying fire from the front and left bank. The fire discipline he also said was excellent, and contributed materially to keeping down the fire from the enemy's sangars.

The enemy's casualties were estimated at some sixty killed and one hundred wounded. Amongst the enemy were some forty of Umra Khan's men, and the fire which Colonel Kelly's force had to face was entirely from Martini-Henry and Snider rifles.

This second success was even greater than the first. All the principal men of the country not employed before the fort of Chitral were present in the action, and the utmost reliance had been placed in the strength of the position. It was therefore a serious blow to the Chitralis when they found that the principal position on the road to Chitral had been summarily captured.

Colonel Kelly halted that night opposite the village of Sanoghar, and on the following day, the 14th of April, marched to Drasan to ascertain the strength of the enemy and his whereabouts, as it was reported that Mohamed Isa had fled in that direction. The road had been broken, and a long detour had to be made up the spur some 2,000 ft. high above the road, necessitating a march of some twenty miles.

The fort at Drasan was found to be unoccupied, and in it were large quantities of grain, which would have been very acceptable to Colonel Kelly had he been able to carry it away, but no transport was available for the purpose as no men could be captured from the neighbouring villages.

The usual road to Chitral runs down the opposite side of the valley to that on which Drasan is situated. It was by this road on the left bank of the river that Captain Ross and Lieutenants Edwardes and Fowler had advanced, and along it the parties under them had been annihilated. The enemy had intended to have arrested Colonel Kelly's progress at or near the spot where Captain Ross's party had suffered so severely, but Colonel Kelly outwitted them by avoiding the terrible defiles on that road and by marching from Drasan high up along the hill-sides on the right bank of the river till he had passed these difficult positions.

In the midst of heavy rain he marched on the 15th of April to Khusht, and on the 16th to Loon; and then on the 17th, being well behind the worst defiles, he descended to the river bed again and crossed the Chitral River to Barnas, though the river at this point is not generally considered fordable, for it is breast-high and runs with rapid current. It was of course with only great risk that men could be taken across, but by linking them together in bands of ten or twelve, and by stationing levies in the stream to help men who might be washed off their legs, and to save kits which might be carried away, Colonel Kelly's force was able to effect the passage of this deep and rapid mountain river. A strategical move of the highest importance had thus been effected and an almost impregnable position turned without the firing of a single shot.

All this time Colonel Kelly had not been able to hear a single word from the garrison in Chitral, nor had he been able to pass a message in to them to give warning of his approach. He was now only two marches distant from Chitral, and the crisis of his arduous march was approaching. This date was indeed the turning-point of the whole campaign—Colonel Kelly had turned the enemy's last position; it was on this day that Lieutenant Harley made his brilliant sortie; and it was on this day Umra Khan was making his last futile effort against General Low's force. The high-water mark of the rebellion had been reached, and from now the tide began to turn rapidly.

On the 18th Colonel Kelly made a short march to Moroi and on the 19th arrived at Koghazi, only one march from Chitral. Here he received his first letter from the beleaguered garrison, and obtained the welcome news that the siege had just been raised and that the enemy had finally fled.

In the afternoon of April 20th the force marched into Chitral and joined hands with their comrades, who had for forty-seven days been invested within the fort.

This famous march of native troops from the plains of India, led by a mere handful of British officers, over a snow-clad range, through precipitous defiles into the heart of a country flushed with successful rebellion, will ever be remembered as a unique exploit of the Indian Army. The news of the success of the little force was soon spread throughout the empire. Everywhere the highest admiration was excited, and critics in the great armies of the Continent joined with ourselves in the praises of the high military qualities which its accomplishment showed that our officers and men possessed. Her Majesty the Queen immediately telegraphed to India her gracious approbation of this remarkable exploit, and the Commander-in-Chief in India, Sir George White, expressed his warm appreciation of the manner in which, in the face of extraordinary difficulties, the advance and operations of the force were conducted, and of the indomitable energy displayed by Colonel Kelly and the officers and troops under his command in overcoming them. The Commander-in-Chief considered the arrangements made for the crossing of the Shandur Pass, the perseverance and skill displayed by the officers, and the excellent behaviour of the troops worthy of the highest praise, and while commending all, recorded especially the important part taken by Captain Borrodaile and his detachment, who were the first over the pass.

A week after Colonel Kelly had reached Chitral Major "Roddy" Owen and myself, riding on ahead of the advanced parties of General Low's force arrived in Chitral. It was a bright sunny day, the country was clothed in all the fulness of spring, the young corn was waving in the fields, the blossoms were forming on the trees and all nature was smiling as we rode through the forty miles of country which separated Chitral from the advance guard which General Gatacre had just led over the Lowarai Pass. But the looks of the people were in striking contrast. Worn, trembling and utterly cowed the Chitralis shrank from even two British officers riding without an escort through their country. It was pitiable to see them. Men, whom a few months before I had seen gay as few but Chitralis in their contented moments can be, were now moving about with careworn faces, thin and exhausted. The people of Chitral had flamed up into rebellion, and were now lying burnt out like the charred remains of a firework. When I asked them why they had been so foolish as to fight us, they wrung their hands and said, "Why were we? We hate these Pathans; they have plundered our houses and carried off our women, but they were strong and close while you were far away, and we never knew you were so powerful as you are. We did not want to fight you, but we were led away."

It was only very few people, however, that we met as we rode through the villages, for most had fled to the hills, believing that General Gatacre's brigade, now just over the Lowarai Pass, was to advance and exact a terrible retribution by massacring them for the space of three days.

Photo Bassano, *Old Bond Street.*

Captain J. McD. Baird.

Company of the 14th Sikhs which formed part of the Garrison of Chitral during the Siege.

Late in the evening of the 27th of April, we rode into Chitral, and had the honour to be the first to congratulate the famous garrison and the officers of Colonel Kelly's force upon their splendid achievements. We found the officers just sitting down to dinner in the very house in which I had lived for many months, and in which Mr. Curzon and I on the previous October had entertained the late Mehtar at dinner. It was situated half-a-mile from the fort, and here we found Sir George Robertson and the other officers, recovered somewhat indeed from what Colonel Kelly's officers had found them, but still looking pale and worn, thin, and with the set, anxious look which had not yet left their faces. They were cheery; they brought out a long-treasured bottle of brandy from the reserve for hospital purposes, and they produced a Christmas plum-pudding which had only that day arrived, and insisted upon our sharing these luxuries with them; but even now they hardly realised that the struggle was yet over, and one or other of them would from time to time go round the sentries posted everywhere round the house.

One of the first subjects on which they spoke to us was about poor Baird. Few officers have ever attached their comrades more sincerely to them than did this brave officer, and he was one of the best and keenest soldiers in the service. He was noted for his tact and for the amiability of his character, and he studied his profession with the spirit of an enthusiast. His coolness was as remarkable as his zeal, and suffering though he was and knowing that he must die, he remained cheerful and collected to the last. He said that he would not have wished to die any other death than the soldier's death which he was now to meet; he had done his duty and led his men as a soldier should do, and he never regretted his fate. He gave a few last messages to those at home and then with a smile on his face and, thinking of his profession to the very end, wished his comrades success in their plans and bade them good-bye.

He died on the morning of the 4th of March, and was buried in the dead of night outside the main gate of the fort while the enemy were firing all round. A little over two months later, when the advance brigade of the Relieving Force arrived in Chitral, General Gatacre read a funeral service over his grave, and Major Aylmer, R.E., who had served together with Baird in the Hunza Campaign three years before and won his Victoria Cross there, erected a tombstone to his memory and with his own hands carved an inscription. His comrades and fellow-countrymen will know then that, far away though he now lies, his grave has not been neglected, but will ever be cared for by the soldiers who follow after him.

After poor Baird I think the subject on which the officers of the garrison spoke most feelingly was the devotion and noble spirit of discipline and determination shown by the Sikhs. There were but a hundred of them in a garrison of nearly four hundred, but the officers said that without them they could never have held out, and that but for these Sikhs not one of them would have been there now. They only grew more enthusiastic as the siege became closer and times seemed harder. With calm self-reliance they stood proudly at bay like a rock with the waves beating against it. And so great was the sense of discipline which their stern old native officer Gurmukh Singh instilled into them, that when during an attack the sick struggled out of hospital to join in the fight he would not excuse even their impulsive bravery, but told them that a soldier's first duty was to obey, that they had been ordered to hospital and there they must stay. It was the discipline ingrained into these men that saved the garrison. As long as a Sikh was on sentry, and while Sikhs were holding a threatened point, Captain Townshend had nothing to fear. The enemy would never catch a Sikh off his guard and could never force their way through a post of Sikhs while one remained alive. They saved the garrison, and the officers gratefully acknowledged their service.

The skill of the enemy was, too, a subject on which the officers specially dwelt. The Chitralis had not previously been considered of much account as a fighting race; but even they, once their blood was up, fought hard and well, and their Pathan allies were as skilful and brave as troops of a regularly-trained army. Umra Khan's men were born warriors; unlike the Chitralis, who by nature prefer polo and sport and dancing to fighting, the Pathans from their childhood upwards think of little else than warfare. They are for ever raiding upon one another, attacking each other's villages, and besieging and defending the forts scattered over their country nearly as thickly as public-houses in England. They therefore showed every ingenuity in the siege of Chitral. To make the most of their ammunition they never fired a shot without clearly making out an object to aim at, and usually with the rifle resting on a stone so as to enable them to aim correctly. The skill which they displayed in the construction of trenches and breastworks to approach the walls; the sagacity they evidenced in repeatedly attacking the water-way and in setting fire to the towers and walls of the fort; and the courage and determination they showed in their attempts to carry out these objects, excited the highest admiration of the besieged.

No less remarkable was their well-directed effort to undermine the walls; and at the close of the siege the defenders found a huge pent roof, which was to have been borne along and placed against the walls of the fort so as to cover the assailants, and huge scaling-ladders, capable of carrying three men abreast. With the aid of these contrivances the enemy had hoped, when the mine had been successfully fired, to have made one last desperate assault upon the devoted garrison before the Relieving Force could arrive. They calculated that the defenders must be getting very short of supplies, for Mr. Robertson in his negotiations with them had always been careful to lead them into this belief. They thought, too, that the native troops must be low at heart, and ready to throw up the sponge at any day. They considered, therefore, that if one great effort could be made they would be able to first crush the Chitral garrison, and then annihilate Colonel Kelly, who they knew had with him only a handful of men with no supplies and no transport to speak of, and who was now in the middle of the worst defiles of the country. But the carefully-planned and brilliantly-executed sortie under Harley had effectually frustrated this last supreme effort of the besiegers, and Colonel Kelly's force had, by their skilful tactics and bravery in action, thwarted the enemy's most cherished plans. Just on the brink of a disaster the British forces came out triumphant; and once again in our fair island's story it was shown that British officers, even though unsupported by a single British soldier, and with only their own stout hearts and strong right arms to trust to, and to the influence they could exercise over men of subject races, had been able to uphold the honour of their race; and the story of the defence and relief of Chitral will be handed down to posterity as one of the most brilliant chapters in the annals of Indian military history.

House occupied by Sher Afzul during the Siege of Chitral Fort.

Now the British Agency.

Printed by Libri Plureos GmbH in Hamburg,
Germany